DAWN
The Doorway

PARENTING
Differently-abled Children

J M MODY

Copyright © 2022 J M Mody.

All rights reserved. No part of this book may be used or reproduced by any means, graphic, electronic, or mechanical, including photocopying, recording, taping or by any information storage retrieval system without the written permission of the author except in the case of brief quotations embodied in critical articles and reviews.

This book is a work of non-fiction. Unless otherwise noted, the author and the publisher make no explicit guarantees as to the accuracy of the information contained in this book and in some cases, names of people and places have been altered to protect their privacy.

Archway Publishing books may be ordered through booksellers or by contacting:

Archway Publishing
1663 Liberty Drive
Bloomington, IN 47403
www.archwaypublishing.com
844-669-3957

Because of the dynamic nature of the Internet, any web addresses or links contained in this book may have changed since publication and may no longer be valid. The views expressed in this work are solely those of the author and do not necessarily reflect the views of the publisher, and the publisher hereby disclaims any responsibility for them.

Any people depicted in stock imagery provided by Getty Images are models, and such images are being used for illustrative purposes only. Certain stock imagery © Getty Images.

ISBN: 978-1-6657-2994-9 (sc)
ISBN: 978-1-6657-2996-3 (hc)
ISBN: 978-1-6657-2995-6 (e)

Library of Congress Control Number: 2022916872

Print information available on the last page.

Archway Publishing rev. date: 11/23/2022

Dawn, the Doorway, Parenting: Differently-abled Children is a nice piece of literature and adroitly describes the life and expectations of parents and children. You have taken due care to understand the psyche and emotions of children with a balanced approach. These children do not anticipate sympathy but expect to treat with love and concern. You have done a commendable task of speaking to the world on their behalf. An overall effort not to hurt them while suggesting ways to heal them and let them live like any other human being. Every reader will appreciate your efforts and will hail you and your book.

I wish you a glorious literary journey and newer milestones

-Dr. Jayant Parikh

Snapshot by the author, a mother seen with her child (Apophenia)

Acknowledgments

*Dedicated to Parents,
Daughter & Granddaughter*

Contact:
dawnthedoorway2022@gmail.com

Preface

The nonfiction memoir Dawn, The Doorway Parenting: Differently-abled Children (Children with congenital anomalies) is a comprehensive, far-reaching book on parenting. It is an all-encompassing, worldwide book for contemporary, present-day carrier-oriented couples and families, especially when a family has a child born with congenital anomaly issues and life-threatening, life-terminating diseases after birth.

Numerous books are written and published routinely by medical and paramedical professionals. Most of those books have specialized medical field terminologies having guidelines and references to advance their medical and paramedical treatment, supported by recently researched information and shared experiences of experts. These are primarily helpful for concerned professionals locally and internationally. These books are usually not referred to by parents for their children's health issues.

Nevertheless, these books have excellent details and are available for present-day parents if they want to read, refer and understand their child's problems to avail of required treatments from medical and paramedical professionals. It may be helpful to parents and family members to support the medical treatments and therapies and actively participate with a better understanding to yield the best possible outcomes for their child.

Dawn, the Doorway primarily alleviates and soothes the dismayed, downcast parents and their immediate family members, having a child born into a family with congenital health issues and life-threatening diseases after birth.

It is to motivate and pursue parents to take special care without feeling discouraged, disheartened, and losing hope while parenting such children. It is to appropriately navigate and boost parents and steadfast immediate family members to have positive attitudes by reassuring their human values to alleviate the child's condition and overall family situation.

It is essential for parents' minds and hearts to develop optimism by understanding the awaited purpose of a child taking birth in a family with congenital anomalies or developing life-threatening diseases. Using convincing hypotheses, J M Mody has attempted to reach parents and other readers with his sincere, enthusiastic, and passionate understanding not to lose hope.

Jayesh has drawn fundamental life values and coupled innovative parenting vision through a resounding, profound hypothesis to perform their required responsibilities with due diligence accepting realities caringly, lovingly, and remaining compassionate towards such a child. He modestly attempts to convey to the parents so they can distinguish and adopt core values of parenting to change for their own better life.

Consequently, the purpose of their taking birth is to harness community building by making homes practice compassion and to pass on the message worldwide. They encourage creating an agreement, a bond between the parents, family members, and dedicated medical and paramedical professionals to unite as team members. It can create a chain; whoever comes in contact with already transformed teammates will motivate and thread further for societal and communal unity and harmony. The goal is to create a lovely caring society to exchange views and opinions to remove disconcertment and judgments on varied subjects.

The goal of writing down is not only to change thinking minds but to touch and feed readers' hearts means writing down to arise and make it transpire. It is an effort to pen down frankly pretty-looking everyday life incidents to persuade readers' hearts with real-life anecdotes and experiences.

Dawn, the Doorway, a memoir, is a personal reflection, the expression of a grandpa as an author to motivate and pursue parents to take special care and attention without feeling disgraced while parenting such children.

Jayesh is confident in reaching readers by inscribing true-life incidents and composing those as worth reading text.

Prologue

Blaire entered the neonatal intensive childcare unit with prayers and confidence that her baby would be fine and she would be happy to welcome her daughter into their lives. It was early morning, the very next day of Dawn's birth.

Christine and Jay had an opportunity to glance through the viewing window and found a healthy-looking baby but then transferred to the neonatal intensive care unit for health issues.

Blaire met a nurse in the corridor who accompanied her to the baby's cradle. Blaire was very anxious, as she had no opportunity to make skin-to-skin contact with or even feed her baby, and she hoped that Dawn would be fine. She wanted to interact with her baby for the first time and to express her gratitude.

The nurse informed her that the baby was primarily clear with meconium and now breathing comfortably. "Good luck," she uttered before getting busy with the other babies.

CONTENTS

01. Distinctive Children 1
    Rejoice with their Genuine Innocence

02. Ascending Opportunities 16
    Nonjudgmental Observers

03. Present-Day Dawn 33
    Plunge into her Lovely World

04. Perturbed Disheartened Blaire 52
    Incredulous at Unforeseen Event

05. Concerns and Sleepless Night 60
    Apprehensive Christine and Jay

06. Cherished Motherhood 68
    Unwavering, Steadfast Routines

07. Blaire Comes Under Trepidation 81
    Family Members Unite to Comfort Blaire

08. Predicament: Vision or Blindness 88
    It could have been Worse

09. Transmit Feelings of Parity 105
    Shared Humility - Practicing Compassion

10. Understand Pain and Suffering 125
    Naturally Born Distinctive Children do not Suffer

11. Stepping towards Doorway: 151
    Discover the Entry to Eternal Contentment

01

Distinctive Children
Rejoice with their Genuine Innocence

In the present-day world, career-oriented couples would like to put extra effort into their jobs during the initial phase of their married life to grow and get established to live happily and comfortably for the years to come. At the same time, they also would like to invite a child into their life to enhance their relationship, creating a lovely, blissful, perfect link between them.

However, sometimes a child is born with congenital lifelong enduring anomalies or develops a life-threatening terminal disease. It is natural for parents to feel terrible and think of shattered dreams when they see a child born with congenital issues or developing life-threatening diseases at a very young age.

They feel loaded with more responsibilities than anticipated having a charming, beautiful regular child, and they may get disheartened and discouraged thinking about managing. They also suddenly realize extra pressure and come under a predicament to change their life priorities to accommodate.

However, when the mother calms down, she realizes her obligatory duties and may cry to relieve her stress, vent deep anguish, and breathe peacefully. Simultaneously, a mother's inner consciousness will stimulate her core value of compassion as she accepts reality and resolves to care for and love her child. She develops a practical and blissful state of mind while looking at her newborn baby's innocence and purity. She understands that her child will need her genuine devotion to life, and she suddenly takes over to be a mother to care for and love her child.

Immediate family members committed to family values may give their assurances of support to such keen and dedicated parents. They all join together to welcome the new arrival child into the family. Unfortunately, some families may not have such support and backing, and those remain ambiguous. Of course, everyone's circumstances and family situations are different. They endure stress, tension, and worry, living a compromised life and accepting unhappiness as part of life.

However, it is not appropriate to accept unhappiness as part of life, as every life is significant, including the newborn child and the parents. Feeling unhappy and downhearted, to begin with, can be understandable, natural, and acceptable.

It is natural for the mother who may feel gloomy and remorseful about this new life; however, she accepts the challenge, trusting her motherhood. It does not matter who assures her and supports her. She makes up her mind to do her best for her child. Consequently, she decides to fulfill her responsibilities to love and care for her child and to feel contented to fill with inner bliss.

Down syndrome typically be diagnosed during pregnancy in the first trimester through ultrasound and immediately after birth. Autism spectrum disorder can appear at eighteen months or even earlier after birth. Simultaneously, a doctor can keep track of a child's developmental history and behavior to diagnose autism and many more health issues.

Some children are born without apparent health issues but develop and are diagnosed with life-terminal diseases like cancer and respiratory and liver diseases. Some are affected aggressively and leave this world at a very young age, while some survive for more extended periods. None of it is under anyone's control.

Consider this a turning point for the better, and one may have to change the complete approach toward life. Once a child with health issues is already born into a family, it is better to be concerned and compassionate. Accept the innocent child's challenges. Perform your best to assist and find opportunities to lead a happy and blissful life together.

Instead of remaining distressed, accept that everything that happens has some purpose. It will be better to start feeling concerned, reassured, comforted, and experience transformation and transcend from within for a better life, leading to a higher stage from within.

It is imperative to understand that every life is precious in this world, and no life should end without having been loved and cared for to the best degree possible by concerned family members. It is mandatory to see that no life should be ignored and be ended abruptly and prematurely, except by its natural course. Regardless of any reason, the mother will feel awful losing a child.

A sensible, moderate way is suggested for parents when they feel entirely encircled by multiple issues, find it awful, and feel insignificant having a child with congenital anomalies or life-threatening disease. The most gentle and blessed approach is to stay positive, perform their best sincerely, and move in the right direction by being virtuous and compassionate. Moreover, find opportunities to ascend towards a doorway to dawn when disappointment and unhappiness completely control life.

Millions of kind-hearted, willing, and compassionate people devote their lives to social services by pursuing medical or paramedical professions, joining the military, and rescuing community services to serve people. Many join organizations, agencies, and NGOs to help children word-wide having congenital anomalies or life-terminating diseases. Ultimately, all these sacrificing, prayerful service persons confirm our journey through evolution to civilization.

Doctors, surgeons, nurses, and therapists do their best to ease health issues and even find a cure with advanced medical science, but in some cases, they remain helpless. Their untiring efforts leading to some success and accomplishments are like a candlelight in the darkness, bringing parents happiness and assuring faith. It is their most human and humble way to serve children, and parents remain gratified.

Children born with lifelong congenital anomalies and those who acquire life-threatening diseases very young are commonly known as *special children*. However, we would recognize them by their characteristic features as naturally *distinctive* or naturally *differently-abled children* in all our further communications.

Everyone has a lovely heart along with a rational mind. Most people in this world are religious and believe in God, have faith in God, and follow their religious beliefs through their faith. We have reasons to believe in God in a different form or as the energy, power, and authority per individual beliefs that precisely monitor the working of the earth and the entire universe.

Some intellectuals act as guides and philosophers, leading communities to make them think and ponder positively by being lovely, caring, and compassionate. Moreover, they have suggested ways to be on humanitarian grounds and score good credits by following life and human values to remain happy and blissful during the present life. There is a reason for every life to visit this beautiful planet. Nothing happens on this planet without reason.

One must accept that we do not control certain aspects of our lives. Recently, the entire world population has gone through the coronavirus pandemic, leading us to understand our status and limitations.

Modern science has yet to find precise and accurate medical reasons for children taking birth with congenital anomalies. Many scientists have researched that congenital abnormalities might be due to genetics, infection, radiation, drug exposure, and, most significantly, for *no known reason*.

Likewise, some naturally distinctive, differently-abled children come out with exceptional performance with the untiring efforts of parents in coordination and cooperation with professional medical staff and therapists. Of course, one can treat such children through advanced medical science to enhance their comfort, increase life expectancy, and act independently for routine activities. On the other hand, some children come out of their own charismatically, shading, superseding their disabilities and deformities to perform incredibly, unbelievably with jaw-lowering performances, which means something has jumpstarted and clicked into their brains. Most of the time, their changes and accomplishments may remain beyond medical science and scientists' conclusions. They become differently abled under *"No specifically, precisely known reason."*

Scientists accept and depend on interpreting religious beliefs and spiritual knowledge when science does not have answers. Of course, they do not leave their works to find solutions, and there are instances where they have found clues and guidelines from religious beliefs and spiritual knowledge.

Similarly, scientists have also unveiled many religious beliefs and understandings as insignificant and unbelievable for religious adherents.

Human life comes with exceptionally incredible, far-fetched powers and energies in this world that require initiation and growth. Unfortunately, after that also, a significant portion remains untapped for most of us.

Nothing happens for no reason. Every life has a reason to visit this beautiful world, and every occurrence has explanations. The arrival of children with congenital anomalies is an issue for medical science; however, they have incredible energies and in-built powers just like their peers. There may be special reasons for their arrival, and they may have unique links, connections, and relations with the eternal truth and overall balancing systems.

With such derivatives, it is essential to understand how and why naturally distinctive, differently-abled children take birth with veiled, hidden powers and have a network with the source energy systems and arrangements.

Children born with congenital anomalies have unique characteristics. One can tap their dynamism for improvements to make them independent to the greatest extent possible, so parents can be comfortable and live their lives without much difficulty. Parents, immediate family members, and other dedicated social servants, doctors, nurses, teachers, and therapists can use such children's hidden powers and characteristics prudently and farsighted to benefit and uplift the children's lives by showing compassion in delivering their services.

Most children with congenital anomalies have excellent, incomparable, unique competence, possibilities, and potential. There are examples of distinctly-abled children who have developed their abilities and aptitudes differently, blending and shading their shortcomings. They have performed excellently, lowering the jaws of bystanders and spectators in various fields, like sports, music, dance, literature, and science.

In most cases, the assistance of positive, optimistic, cheerful parents, physical therapists, immediate family members, teachers, and trainers make these children feel appreciated and worthy. Moreover, they can gain the confidence and assurance of being taken care of, looking at and comparing their performances with others despite their shortcomings.

Science and technology have made tremendous, unimaginable progress through inventions and discoveries. They have lifted many curtains to reveal existence's veiled powers and energies and use those for our comfort and convenience. They also experienced that the more they lifted the curtain, the more mysteries would remain to unfold. Something new to resolve will erupt, and the entire process will continue.

The findings and new inventions have won people's faith, but looking at the vast number of unveiled mysteries of our existence, we cannot be entirely safe and secure that we have mastery. However, they do not get discouraged and keep working on alternatives for humankind.

We are part of the entire existence and nature, and one who understands nature, reality, and charismatic events will realize how beautifully everything balances naturally. Suppose something undesirable happens in one's life despite knowledge and precautions taken; it's a sign and confirmation that we are part of it and cannot control it. The process of natural self-governing is a part of the vast universe and will continue until the entire system crashes to restart.

Whatever we make use of modern equipment and instruments, healthcare accessories, modes of transportation, and many more for our comfort and convenience and a better living need regularly scheduled maintenance, precise calibration, and tests to remain in operation and continue getting services. Against all such arrangements and systems, think about different natural systems and displays, including the universe's solar system, which meticulously keeps running.

While using natural treasures, we remain ignorant and do everything possible to increase our comfort and convenience, forgetting any adverse effects on its balance and working. We do all possible activities by becoming self-centered. However, most of those disturbances get readjusted and recalibrated through self-governing balancing systems. Nature always tries to absorb all such changes and maintains its operating systems.

Thanks to science and technology, we have sufficient information about the planet on which we live. Scientists know that the earth's spin axis tilted at 23.5 degrees while moving into orbit around the sun, creating days and nights and different seasons for us. For millions of years, there has been no change in this position. If the tilting angle changes slightly, most of the land portion will come underwater, sink, and most lives will be jeopardized or finished.

When a child is born with congenital anomalies, it is natural for parents to experience restrictions to their living life and progress in the material world and their freedom to enjoy worldly affairs. We feel pain and unhappiness when someone is not as per our desires and demands. Of course, the parents' dream of having a lovely child, as per their definitions, shatters, and they may get discouraged.

However, better options are always available than remaining unhappy and disheartened and deciding to live a compromised life.

One should not forget that once any woman becomes a mother, she is empowered to deal with her child's life eventualities. It is a prerequisite for parents to set model roles while caring for their children compassionately. Opportunities are always available through such distinctive children to lead a divine, contented, and blissful spiritual life. Don't panic, but understand and accept that they may have to change their thinking to lead a happy and blissful life is essential.

According to research, about 3 to 4% of children are born with congenital anomalies in the United States of

America. A congenital disability in one of every thirty-three children born means more than 100,000 babies in the United States annually. About eight million newborns are born annually with congenital disabilities globally, of which around 300,000 die due to associated complications. An estimated 6% of babies worldwide are born with congenital anomalies.

Congenital malformations happen during the gestation period, the development of the fetus before birth. In other words, we can say that about ninety-seven out of a hundred babies born in the United States arrive without significant congenital disabilities, such as spina bifida or Down syndrome.

Congenital disabilities are mainly of two types. Children are born with structural disorders, in which problems are apparent by the shape of the body part. Another segment where they are born has functional disorders, including metabolic and degenerative diseases.

Women who are thirty-five years or older at the time of delivery, i.e., advanced maternal age, have a greater risk of having an infant with a chromosomal abnormality like Down syndrome.

A women's peak reproductive years are from the late teens to the late twenties. By age thirty, fertility starts to decline. This decline is more rapid when women reach thirty-five years of age, and by forty-five, fertility declines so much that getting pregnant naturally is unlikely.

There are four leading causes of congenital disabilities. Most are genetic. One or more genes might change or have a mutation that prevents them from working as planned, designed, and determined. There can be chromosome problems or exposure to high doses of medicines, chemicals, or other toxic substances, creating issues and infections during pregnancy. Furthermore, there may be a lack of certain nutrients.

Certain congenital anomalies are taken care of by knowing in advance during pregnancy and avoiding a child born with gene malfunctions by terminating a pregnancy. In some cases, relief through treatments and therapies makes life comfortable, while most are not curable and may show severe syndromes with growth. The most common, severe congenital anomalies are heart defects, neural tube defects, and Down syndrome. Congenital anomalies may result from genetic, infectious, nutritional, or environmental factors, and it is often difficult to identify the exact causes.

A child may be born with lifelong, enduring anomalies and life-threatening ailments, including Down syndrome, autism, and many other life-terminating health issues. Present-day advanced science has not identified the exact causes for all of these. Through more research, science may progress, but other related problems may show up by the time they come out with solutions. As discussed, sometimes scientists may have to depend on interpreting religious beliefs and spiritual knowledge when science does not have answers.

Blaire and Ryan had planned to invite a child into their life, creating a lovely, blissful, perfect link between them to feel comfortable and live a happy life. Blaire became pregnant and worked more hours to get enough money for the home. It was obligatory to plan and save more money for a new arriving baby and to make everyone comfortable.

Unfortunately, Blaire could not know in advance about Dawn arriving with congenital anomalies, as obstetricians could not detect it during routine checkups, especially during pregnancy. It is rare, but it does happen in some cases.

The arrival of Dawn with congenital deformities changed Blaire and Ryan's life priorities. Immediate family members promised to assist with this unexpected situation. Christine and Jay had decided to support and remain committed for the initial crucial years.

In this situation, any mother would do her best to give her child the best possible life with her health-related shortcomings. Blaire needed to continue to be a prime income earner, the source for the family. She had a chance to get a promotion at her job, and with the changed circumstances, she welcomed to increase in the inflow of money.

Blaire decided to acquire additional professional skills and knowledge to deal with Dawn, and she did it. Initially, she faced some issues concentrating and justifying her input at her job.

However, she won the confidence of colleagues and higher-ups with such added commitments at home and balanced it nicely.

Blaire also realized that her professional career should not be disturbed and affected, as she would need much more money to survive comfortably with such a child.

Having developed serenity and blissfulness within looking at their child, Blaire and Ryan realized Dawn would need genuine devotion from them in performing obligatory responsibilities.

02

Ascending Opportunities
Nonjudgmental Observers

A child with congenital anomalies can be a dawning, a beginning, to ascend in the present life and to score for better placement for the parents and the entire team. Their characteristic abnormalities and deformities become catalysts to restore love, care, and compassion in parents. Furthermore, parents and caretakers can feel reaffirmation and reassurance of being caring, compassionate human beings.

Distinctive children lead introverted lives; however, they act as observers, surveyors, witnesses, and navigators. They create a foundation, laying a platform for the commencement to develop understanding and rise to score for upliftment in life. They are the spring source and can trigger flow, buoyancy, and resilience in the parents and all concerned. They give parents and other caretakers an unspoken, implied, an indirect invitation to plunge into their world of innocence and purity and rise with selfless love and compassion. It is an opportunity to accept the offered boon, and experience the transformation, transcend to ascend to the afterlife.

Every human is born pure and innocent but grows to mature with learning and personal experiences, evolving into a different person. Most adapt to change quickly to gain worldly benefits in abundance by becoming greedy and self-centered. They remain unhappy with increased desires and demands and thirst for peace and inner blissfulness. Eventually, they suffer from the reverse effects, the feeling of dissatisfaction constantly.

Differently-abled children are also born pure and innocent. They maintain uniqueness and originality with growth and remain sinless and incorruptible. They hardly change quickly to gain worldly benefits by becoming greedy and selfish. They do not adopt any shortcuts with their growth and development, even though most exhibit appreciable changes with exclusive bringing-up, therapies, training, and teaching. It encourages parents, immediate family members, therapists, trainers, and teachers to continue without discouragement. Of course, they are born with distinctive, differently-abled characteristics, and some may show splendid performance and accomplishment.

The differently-abled child comes into this world with incredible energy, like any other person, but needs initiation. At the same time, they also remain catalysts for parents to grab opportunities to be humane and filled with human life values.

Some children adopt positive changes with their parents, therapists, and caretakers' untiring efforts, which become a bonanza for them to remain motivated and hopeful. Their unique characteristics also indirectly encourage them to complete their assignments and offer the opportunity to ascend to a better life.

Distinctive children are not commonly placed persons; however, they keep coming, appearing routinely. Along with introverted characteristics, they remain anticipated, prearranged observers. Parents shouldn't consider them unfortunate to have a distinctive child; however, they should stay involved, dedicated, and compassionate while caring for their child.

Life and human values are essential commodities for human communities, and these children are the route to achieving those. In short, these children are one of the means to adopt harmony within the family and between communities, so parenting a child with congenital anomalies makes a home practice compassion. Practicing compassion is a prerequisite for the establishment of humanity in this world.

Love, care, and compassion are powerful tools and have played a significant role in ancient civilizations and can play an essential role in the families and communities of the present world. Compassion is not a relationship between the caretakers, healers, and sufferers; compassion is a deeply rooted perception in human awareness.

With compassion, a person becomes aware of another person's suffering, feels empathy for the same, and takes positive actions to ease, alleviate, and lessen such suffering by being a lovely human being. When treated compassionately, a person will not feel sad even looking at shortcomings and will remain joyful.

Much research is going on to study compassion with the human mind and heart through neuroscience, psychology, literature, spirituality, civilization, and theology, which may be significant to the very existence of humankind and the environment we share with our entire existence.

According to the hypothesis, children born with congenital deformities and disabilities have unbelievable hidden powers and a great network with the source energy systems and arrangements. They have divine goals and aims to increase humanism, spiritual divinity, and a celestial point of view for all persons concerned and involved, including parents and immediate family members. With such regard, they arrive in the family as anticipated distinctive observers and inspirers to draw parents and other caring, resonant, lovely, dedicated souls to join as teammates in opening doorways to the Dawn.

Ecological balance is a biological term used to describe an ecosystem where different species coexist to create a sustainable environment. Plants and animals depend upon each other for their survival. The natural balances are made possible through self-governing, ecological, climactic, and atmospheric systems.

Our planet and the entire universe have many autonomous, self-governing, self-operating systems. Some of those systems have been in operation for millions of years. These systems work so routinely, gently, and meticulously that we hardly notice and feel their existence, working, and importance.

We have intelligent brains compared to other lifeforms. Compared to other fauna and flora, we have understood more quickly to learn adaptation and ways to use naturally available infrastructure to safeguard and be comfortable in our existence. We have developed further and have gone through an evolution, followed by civilization.

Demonstrative intelligence skills can be a prerequisite for the development of empathy. These involve the ability to positively understand, use, and manage our emotions to relieve stress, communicate effectively, empathize with others, and overcome challenges. One can build self-evaluation upliftment for oneself, and each particular act of compassion can have far-reaching effects.

In other words, distinctive children come to initiate thresholds for entrance, elevate human life, and act as anticipated, designated, differently-abled observers, onlookers, and witnesses. Their arrival is a part of a self-governing, self-operating balancing system in the world of human beings.

Children born with congenital anomalies and children who acquired life-threatening diseases reciprocate the services rendered to them and the devotion offered by parents, immediate family members, therapists, and many more who join the team. It is the natural balancing system of humanity and human values to achieve and maintain an equilibrium, stable state like homeostasis. Homeostasis is a technical term used in biology, physiology, and psychology, meaning the tendency of an organism to maintain internal stability or a group of organisms to act cooperatively.

They visit with specially designed and assigned jobs as distinguished onlookers, distinctive observers, and witnesses. Their arrival as naturally and uniquely talented children, with their characteristics becoming catalysts to inspire and stimulate parents and team members for their emergence of Dawn by being compassionate human beings and maybe navigating for better placement life after. They come so naturally that some people take them casually and make mistakes in recognizing them.

The naturally distinctive children have the characteristics of differently-abled children who come to connect with such a beautiful system that they may not be aware of their unique assignment as designated observers to remain unbiased and perform successfully. Furthermore, they come with different drives and influences with changed genetic programming to be more effective.

Some children have unusual symbolic appearances, strange and unexpected behaviors, and various unpredictable emotions, actions, and gestures. They come with deformities, disabilities, and shortcomings; according to medical science, they are considered incapable, incompetent, and different. They witness without offering comment, criticism, appreciation, or justification to their parents and even to self-sacrificing, dedicated, steadfast, committed immediate family members and many other caretakers, trainers, therapists, and teachers.

They remain witnesses and observers and feed their reports into self-governing, naturally operated balancing systems for further scrutiny, evaluation, and conclusions. Their feeding information to the system will be without analytical analysis, review, and critique, so they must report by remaining unbiased and nonjudgmental.

These distinguished children, as observers, indirectly provide a platform for parents, steadfast, committed, caring family members, and therapists to prepare themselves to live with awareness, responsiveness, genuine compassion, and emotional dedication to perform obligatory responsibilities and provide special needs services as caretakers. In response to such acts of concerned people, these children offer the opportunity to them to alleviate, ascend, and upgrade themselves by being kind and compassionate.

Their prime purpose and goals are to prepare and uplift well-performing parents and teammates to ascend the mystic source ladder of divine spiritual life. These distinctive children also indirectly inspire, stimulate, and create selfless bonds of altruistic, philanthropic self-sacrificing love and care for parents and teammates. They encourage creating an agreement, a bond between parents, family members, and dedicated service persons to unite as team members.

The transformation will jumpstart once a parent or family member accepts the offer as a boon and acts appropriately. They transcend within themselves and experience blissfulness and fulfillment while caring for such children. They also become catalysts to create explicit passages to restore love, care, and compassion in the beautiful world.

They offer an opportunity to all concerned to upgrade by being good human beings filled with human values of caring, loving, and compassion. With the presence of a distinctive child, the home should become an everyday school to practice compassion, and it is the most practical way. It will also indirectly be helpful for community-building.

Consequently, parents and family members also can get uplifted as per their religious beliefs for the afterlife, salvation, paradise, moksha, nirvana, and many more. There is no point in picking at the differences between what one believes and what others do not. Every religion can navigate a path of salvation by understanding its core values correctly and avoiding misinterpretation and misconception. The purpose is to find treasures and stay positive for humanity and well-being, as anyone can achieve through the most innocent child.

As per the hypothesis, children born with congenital deformities and disabilities offer opportunities through self-governing systems. Moreover, they encourage parents, concerned immediate family members, and connected people to be caring, loving, and compassionate. They balance humanity, human and life values within the family, community, and world.

At the same time, persons of intellectual wisdom keep trying to create balance through conferences, debates, religious philosophy, sermons, religious gatherings, and many more ways and means. Recently, the coronavirus pandemic has reminded us to understand human beings' limitations by creating a lockdown of the entire world, including prayer places, for months and years.

Children severely affected by congenital issues may not find differences in having the company of another child within the family, which is an entirely different situation. However, these children remain engrossed in their world but do not make the mistake of taking them for granted. Their brains may catch frequencies with powerful, potent receptors to perform as observers. They can capture required data to complete their assignment as an observer for the self-governing balancing system to complete their part of the job.

Under the circumstances, a question arises: Can they observe as per the hypothesis and feed their observation to a self-governing natural balancing system of humanity?

To understand the hypothesized theory, we may try to understand routine present-day lifestyles. We keep an electronic device within the home to have instant information, stay updated, and sometimes answer queries. We frequently ask for some information, and related information may get registered in their systems, and next time we get quick, desired associated answers.

Related items, commercials, or information may pop up on a personal laptop, iPhone, and iPad screen when we browse for some other things. It may also happen accidentally that some product information pops up while working on the internet, links get opened by mistake, and the hub registers, follow up to catch us. We ask for specific product information in our browsing; subsequently, we may have discussed it within the home.

Scientists discover, invent, and develop modern equipment and instruments for comfort and convenience. However, they ultimately use natural resources, and the entire system depends on natural atmospheric mediums for effective operation. If the atmosphere is not clear for transmitting, broadcasting, and conducting media, we have difficulties operating electronic devices with adverse weather effects.

Scientists have known our brain as a super-unimaginable, highly compound composite computer system. It is rare, but when a disturbance occurs in regular patterns of chromosomes, a child develops gene malfunctions during pregnancy and will have congenital issues. However, some are born more severely affected than others.

Human beings are born with a pair of eyes for vision, ears for hearing, kidneys for excretion, and lungs for breathing. It is evident that when one fails, the second takes up a load of its work which we observe even when someone becomes disabled with one physical body part like a leg or arm. We use only a meager portion of the brain, and unimaginable stored power can remain veiled, concealed, and unused.

It is like an iceberg. The tip of the iceberg is one-tenth of its portion outside the ocean's surface. A substantial part of the iceberg remains underwater and unseen. We do not mistake the iceberg's unseen, unveiled portion as not in existence. Whatever exposed portion we see of the iceberg may not have its core portion, a powerful center. Its core is underwater, and the iceberg's existence depends on that powerful balancing center.

Similarly, the human brain has significant hidden unveiled power, which may have integral core characteristics. It may also have hidden, unused, veiled vitalities and energies, so one cannot take the unveiled portion of the brain as not existing, a dump or a junkyard. Scientists may come out in the future through untiring research to support such a hypothesis, and differently-abled children and many more may be beneficiaries of such outcomes.

In the case of severely affected children through congenital anomalies or children developing life-threatening, terminating diseases, even those who become unconscious or enter into a coma remaining unconscious do perform their duties as observers. They minimally react or show no reactions to parents, other caretakers, or medical or paramedical service persons. They remain at a minimum level in their activities, and most of the time, they stay in their mood and world. Under the same hypothesis, they appear around family members and others but remain almost isolated from them, and on the other hand, they may remain joined with self-governing systems.

However, with all the above, differently-abled or severely affected children or a child with life-threatening life termination may have an activated, charged brain portion that may not be similar to a typical child. Thus, correspondingly, the brain portions may get triggered under a self-governing balancing system, which commonly remains unused.

Thus, the unused portion of the brain of differently abled or severely affected children may be acting as a receptor or reflector, unconsciously or obligatorily, for their special duty of observation.

In such a case, the unveiled, unused brain portion receives observations as a receptor or acts as a reflector to transmit to a self-governing natural system. In a way, we see a child occasionally swing some portion of the body and hang his head to collect and reflect observed data with the system. Sometimes, we find them sitting in a quiet position to receive data through a particular portion of the brain, which acts as a reflector and sends reflection to the self-governing system. Thus, severely affected children are also effectively working to meet their responsibilities to a self-governing balancing system and job completion. They need not analyze or prepare a consolidated report with comments while sending it to the pool or hub.

Do we need to doubt that human brain capacities and capabilities may not develop appropriate systems for severely affected children having congenital anomalies?

If we look with a bit of insight and broad thinking, we will find a win-win situation. A family with a distinctive child can be found in every corner of the world, regardless of race, religion, caste, creed, wealthy or low-income family, literate or illiterate, and those motivate parents and members of the immediate family to be lovely, caring, and compassionate persons. It is not the only way to transform and establish a beautiful world filled with loving people; however, it can be one of the excellent ways and means.

The naturally distinctive children come from such a beautiful system that they may not be aware of their unique assignment as designated observers to remain unbiased and nonjudgmental to perform successfully.

They come with distinctly different influences and drives with changed genetic programs for medical science researchers to go into detail and find their significance as nothing happens unnecessarily. Every life has its purpose on this planet.

Children are born into a family at the parents' invitation. When they come with specific characteristics and traits, mainly congenital deformities and disabilities, love, and care for them with an unwavering sense of commitment are obligatory. It is to be kept in mind that while taking care of them, please do not show feelings of kindness, pity, and mercy towards them. Please don't feel misfortune, disappointment, or even shame while caring for them, as it will be an insult and humiliation after knowing and identifying them under the hypothesis.

It is vital how one thinks and absorbs the realities of others. An unknown person unintentionally may feel pity looking at such a child's parents and immediate family members. At the same time, some other person may feel stirred and driven to compassion, and the scene can be a triggering point to bring changes in his life. It is essential to treat these children with developed understanding and inner core concerns and remain motivated and inspired to be on the path by being compassionate.

We need to perform our requisite responsibilities. These children also come at our invitation and do not come empty-handed, especially when they come with congenital issues. They come with a valuable return gift: the implied guiding force for our betterment. They appear as the sufferers but hardly suffer, which we will discuss in further communications.

Nothing precious comes to anyone without sacrifice, devotion, unwavering steadfast commitments, and tremendous effort. Dealing with distinctive, differently-abled children is an opportunity offered or is a boon to upgrade self by being a lovely, caring, compassionate person. A home becomes a place to practice compassion, and a very caring person can influence many more, which is one of the ways and means to make a lovely community and a planet. How can we justify evolution without being transformed and transcended by being civilized, compassionate, comforting, and caring as uplifted human beings?

Every child is lovely, the highest gift ever offered by nature to this world. Discussing and considering children born with congenital anomalies with an autonomous, self-governing system does not mean we compare them with our consecrated holy messiahs, messengers, and avatars. It is primarily for parents and their immediate family members not to get disheartened and discouraged and not to curse innocent children under different misunderstood and misconceived religious beliefs about children born with congenital deformities and disabilities.

There is no intention to offend or hurt anyone's beliefs and sentiments, only to motivate and navigate concerned persons toward humanity and acceptance for such children and to establish worldwide compassionate communities.

The innocent attention-grabbing, mystical, blessed look of a newly born child may shade or escape the parents' attention for its congenital disabilities. It is challenging to differentiate some congenital disabilities by physically observing and concluding anything for them immediately after birth.

Once again, it is not to encounter medical science and expert professionals and their routine procedures for a newborn child. It is not to ignore professionals' untiring job responsibilities; without those, what we comfortably enjoy health care today may not have been enjoying.

Every religious philosophy has appreciated childhood innocence and purity, but then after having experienced worldly affairs, these children are found changing with maturity as an adaptation. Furthermore, these changes may help them deal with and manage this big and tricky material world.

Naturally, distinctive children are born with inherent, intrinsic characteristics and factors. They offer a ladder to ascend and uplift humanity to their parents, caretakers, medical staff, teaching and training staff, and many more. They have a specific assignment as observers to witnesses by being unbiased and nonjudgmental.

It is all implied, indirect intuition they provide, and one can say they indirectly act as navigators with their beautiful innocent smiles. A charismatic smile leads every concerned person to find the fascinating world within them.

03

Present-Day Dawn
Plunge into her Lovely World

It is a typical, familiar scene in the home during morning sessions where everyone becomes busy. Every person wants to get ready to go to work to earn and bring home a livelihood. Even school-going children quickly prepare to go to school; some may have to attend extracurricular activities, coaching classes, and much more. The home looks like a tiny robotic world in the morning session, as everyone knows what to do without wasting time which they routinely perform five days a week.

Despite that, all appear tensed and stressed, as they must match their schedules, go out, and perform to the best of their abilities in their respective fields.

The nuclear family concept of developed countries has also become popular in developing and underdeveloped countries. Parents needed to hand over their preschool children, including infant babies, to the childcare center, daycare center, or caretakers available at home.

With the nuclear family concept, parents do not have responsible persons available at home to take over their unfinished jobs of the morning routines and to go out comfortably for their commitments. A time slot for unscheduled work becomes challenging unless it sounds like an emergency. Besides, the situation becomes more difficult for a family having a child with congenital anomalies.

The atmosphere at home becomes happy and full of fun, in the evening, especially for the children. It is understandable for children to feel good when parents return home from their jobs. Dawn also eagerly waits to see everyone back home. She always dreams and makes beautiful plans for something different to do with the family after dinner.

Commuting remains more tiring for people due to heavy traffic, especially those returning from downtown. Blaire was working at a New York hospital, and returning home to Jersey City from New York was tiresome. While returning home, she recalls and thinks about Dawn and sometimes some of her office incidents, the behavior of noncooperative patients while giving them physical therapy, next-day job pressures, and scheduled meetings, which put her under stress.

Under all such circumstances, she must make up her mind to connect with family members and keep a happy and entertaining mood for herself and others once she returns home.

It was natural that Dawn wanted her parents' attention to talk about her daily activities and accomplishments in the classroom and on the playground. Of course, Blaire interacts nicely with Dawn by expressing her concerns and asking for the entire day's activities to make her feel good and to balance her absence by questioning and understanding any issues.

Blaire worked hard to teach, train, and arrange all possible facilities for required therapists to accomplish Dawn to today's well-groomed stage and make her independent of most of the routines. Being a physical therapist and working at a decent level at the hospital, she has also molded herself for Dawn, like a prime therapist at home. Dawn is in seventh grade and studying at a regular public school with all the other students.

It is a typical scene, the situation of the present-day family in the evening, to remain engrossed with TV shows and films and involved in personal electronic devices like iPhones and iPad. It is natural for parents to come home tired and exhausted after a day's work, find a cozy corner, and be involved in entertaining and relaxing activities to divert from a monotonous, stressful day.

It was routine for Blaire to change her job attire after retiring from the day's work, be comfortable, switch on music or TV to follow their regular serial episodes, and feel relaxed at home.

It was evident that Dawn remained upset during the evening, as she could not participate in watching TV shows due to her vision and hearing impairments. Moreover, she became upset when everyone tried to convince her to sit and enjoy TV programs.

Sometimes, everyone remains so engrossed while watching TV shows that they keep increasing the volume to enjoy music beats, catch the lyrics, and even listen to the dialogue. They forget about the person who uses hearing aids for routine communication. The calibrated hearing devices are for specific sound wavelengths and good pitches for comfort. Dawn loves to be with her iPad, as she can keep adjusting its volume according to requirements for different types of shows.

Having realized such probable possibilities with hearing-aid calibration, we understood why Dawn never wanted to be in the family room when other family members enjoyed viewing big-screen TV shows. We realized her non-preference and irritation and understood her annoyance with particular sound frequencies. We learned about her disliking of sensitivity; someone was tapping a spoon on the bowl at the dining table. The lack of ability to reduce sensitivity becomes a challenging factor. We can say such children may build something related to misophonia if not cared for and treated in time.

Looking at Dawn's genuine difficulties, we decided not to switch on the TV unless she went to her bedroom after dinner. It was difficult for everyone, as TV is the most common entertainment, and we all could gather for talk and entertainment after dinner.

Blaire thought to resolve such an issue so that everyone could watch TV shows and Dawn could sit with everyone. She need not go to her room to avoid sound disturbances and remain alone on the upper floor and feel deserted. Blaire browsed and searched for iPad programs of Dawn's interest. Those programs were action-packed and captivating, and she could remain fully engaged without the soundtrack. Blaire also wanted Dawn to occasionally glance at TV programs to create a habit and develop a vision for distant sights.

Dawn was happy to unplug and remove her hearing aids, and the rest of the family members could continue their TV programs. With such an innovative introduction, Dawn could sit with her family and be around family members in the family room for the evening session.

It was okay and acceptable for a couple of days; however, Dawn felt uncomfortable without hearing aids, and dejectedly, she would go to the upper floor to be in her room. It was just for experimenting, but it didn't work, and then TV viewing was also restricted for two hours to comfort Dawn; furthermore, Blare realized Dawn's concern.

Blaire always remains focused on Dawn and understands her discomforts and dislikes. Blaire accompanies Dawn to her room and remains engaged in talking to her on different subjects so as not to keep her from feeling ignored and neglected. Blaire makes sure Dawn gets busy, which makes her happy.

Once Dawn is happily involved with her activities and feels comfortable, then with her permission, Blaire comes back for TV programs if those are of her interest. Otherwise, she remains around Dawn until she sleeps to make her feel good.

We realized Dawn and Blaire's unhappiness with leaving the family room where TV and music shows are on for all other family members' entertainment. These may appear as minor issues but have tremendous adverse impacts when a home has a child with congenital anomalies.

Electronic devices are friendly for child development, but only if used for that purpose and not to kill boredom. It is essential to ensure they do not replace their friends and enjoy playing with them and involvement with family members and pets at home.

A naturally distinctive, differently-abled child having no other child in the house to interact or play with may feel isolated. Parents need to be more attentive, but the scenario remains much better when more than one child is in the home. A child needs the company of another child to keep talking and playing, and they remain engrossed in their world; otherwise, complaining about boredom remains a standard feature.

The second child may be an adopted child or a family-born child. It is essential to nurture and cultivate liking and affection in a child to remain associated with a distinctive child. There are chances that a second child, the adopted or family-born child, will find the company of other children, schoolmates, and community friends more appealing, and that can be obvious too. At the same time, they become uninterested in being with the distinctive child.

Creating an attachment, a bond of love, care, and understanding, is essential, especially in the adopted child, for a distinctive child to serve the purpose. It is required to create a great combo between them as a team; otherwise, this remains only temporary relief for the distinctive child, who may feel deserted later. Children severely affected by congenital issues may not find differences in having the company of another child, which is an entirely different situation. The adopted child unknowingly turns ignorant, defeating the adoption's purpose.

It was essential for Dawn not to remember and come out with her impairments and feel terrible. One fine day, while sitting next to her and watching TV programs in the family room, I deliberately thought to share my difficulties with her and said,

"Dawn, look, Grandpa has high-powered eyeglasses and cannot see clearly. He also has hearing issues, especially catching the dialogue on TV, and it worsens when someone from family cross-talks in between."

I behaved purposefully, having similar challenges and problems. Christine and Blaire also got involved and seconded. They wanted to encourage my communication with Dawn, and to make it more effective, they both jumped up and made a fun mockery of her grandpa.

"Dawn, it is true," said Christine.

"Grandpa does not understand, cannot listen to the dialogue, and does not have a clear vision. However, he sits in the family room to be with family members. Otherwise, he may have to miss the opportunities to interact with all of us."

And Blaire affectionately clarified,

"Dawn, it is family time. We will adjust our volume to make you comfortable, but be around with family."

Dawn came out with a good smile and shared high-fives with everyone. She also hugged me as a teammate, and from that day onward, we created a Granddaughter Grandpa Team. It was fun to watch Dawn's happiness during such discussions.

It was essential to discuss and highlight grandpa's difficulties and shortcomings to convey feelings of equality to Dawn and console and soothe her by understanding that it is not that she only has such issues and her issues are also not severe. Parents and immediate family members need to explain to such children that everyone has some problems and can't be like the superheroes of comic books and adventure books. Hence, they need not feel wrong about their shortcoming. It is to make them feel at parity.

After that, Dawn became busy with her iPad, which was an opportunity to explain to Blaire & Christine,

"It is essential to transmit feelings and connect with Dawn so that her relationship is with equals. It must come out as shared humanity."

Moreover, as I explained to Blaire and Christine,

"Unless one develops concern and compassion by realizing Dawn's difficulties and sufferings by being with her, one cannot understand her issues. Even Dawn will not be comfy with all communications and actions. Furthermore, we changed the subject, and it was a great scene of laughing, joking, giving high-fives, and hugging each other. It was great contentment for everyone looking at her confidence and happiness.

Dawn said to her mother,

"Look, it is not only me; Grandpa is the same as her."

She was proud to tag me as her best friend, Bestie. It was a great approval and pleasure to all of us that we could reach Dawn. She again got busy with her iPad, and we continued our discussion.

We started to understand more clearly the issues that keep coming up in her life like she could not run fast or jump with a long leap to avoid a small puddle of sprinkler water on the walkways. It was essential for Dawn to learn to balance her body even though she had issues with vision. We gave her practice by holding her hand to walk on the roadside curbing so that she could come out from fear. We made her participate and practice playing hopscotch. It was fun to watch her happiness with such small accomplishments.

"While playing with friends in the evening, she could not connect and kick a ball easily or even ride an electric scooter independently," Blaire added, "She may also be finding difficulties in school during sports activities."

Most of the time, we make her feel like a winner. It was essential to encourage Dawn, so we pretended all such activities were otherwise challenging for anyone.

After knowing that we all were at par with her, she got excited to take on the challenges, and when she achieved those, she felt elevated and better. We realized it was the most straightforward to make a child or grandchild happy and accept shortcomings.

Practicing first as teammates, co-players, and partners was essential. After that, when her turn came, we helped her complete the challenge and ensured she did well on the first attempt. It was important not to miss any opportunity to teach her something she enjoyed which was helpful to her. We made her realize that she has improved, which made her happy and encouraged, and she remained boosted to practice again, maintaining her interest.

Thus, we enjoyed being like her and being buddies. She felt happy, and we enjoyed creating our unique world of sameness.

At home, we also took special care of her to increase her confidence. We served food in a deep soup plate for dinner instead of a flat dinner plate, a regular dish. It made her happy and comfortable plugging and dragging food using a fork or spoon and supporting it with another spoon or knife without spilling it out while dining. It made her feel that she knew her table manners and did not spill food like her grandpa. It always boosted her confidence by forgetting her shortcomings.

We keep napkins and a glass of water ready for her use, as sometimes she needs them while eating, which gives her a feeling of being taken care of, and if she spills food by any chance before she notices, we purposely spill food to provide her with feelings of equality. Moreover, we both practice eating without spilling the food simultaneously.

Whenever grandma Christine cooks the food of her choice, she remains around until her grandma offers her some food items to taste. She makes sure to serve food with a proper dish-out on my desk, waits until I taste, eat, and conveys lovely thanks to her. Christine knows she did not eat even though she used to inquire about the food taste purposefully and grumble. Moreover, when her grandma complains that Dawn never shares with her, we all enjoy laughing.

Dawn also enjoys teasing her grandma by expressing her lovely concerned feelings, saying she loves to share with grandpa being a best friend.

Christine and I used to feel gratified looking at Dawn's joy, the privileged friendly platonic innocent relationship, and we remain thankful to God for her arrival in the family. We both feel fortunate as we got to live and stay associated with her.

It was all blessing in disguise to see Dawn growing, gaining the required understanding and maturity close to her other cousins and friends.

It was noticeable that sometimes Dawn felt bored during virtual school, sitting alone in her study room and watching the teacher and other boys and girls interacting.

Dawn mainly has vision and hearing issues, and she manages with high-powered glasses & hearing aids. Even though it was great to see her active participation during virtual classes, the teachers appreciated her interest and involvement, giving her the required attention.

Blaire resolves her titbit school difficulties after coming home from work without feeling tired. During weekends and job off days, she teaches her to revision of school studies and to keep updated on next week's subjects.

Virtual schools have advantages and disadvantages for everyone, including children and parents. These vary from family to family, considering their circumstances. However, one thing was sure: most students missed their friends and the freedom to be out of the home. Even commuting from home to school and back with friends gives them happiness.

Grandpa and Grandma remained engrossed with Dawn during the day, which helped her stay busy and feel good. Dawn felt happy and contented about getting assistance when she faced difficulties operating the computer during her virtual study of the coronavirus pandemic.

It was fun to assist Dawn with her loud and straightforward call to seek help from the upper floor study room whenever she got stuck with the computer program and could not resolve it independently. At the same time, before I reached her to solve issues, Christine always made sure to give a second call as a reminder of Dawn's call, so I had to rush to her room to resolve her problems.

I could resolve the issue most of the time, but sometimes it was not easy. Whenever such a problem arose, most of the time, it was a disconnection from the classroom or disturbances in connection. It used to be like an emergency to find the problem and reestablish connectivity quickly so Dawn did not miss her teachings. After having experienced it a couple of times, I knew if I asked her some operating-related questions, she used to get some clues and take over, solving independently.

It was a great satisfaction to look at her happiness when I being her grandpa, could not solve the issue, and she used to feel more intelligent and quicker than Grandpa. Ultimately, all such incidences gave her a feeling of likeness and sameness.

Watching Dawn repeating and narrating an entire day's different incidents for her mom was great fun when she returned from her job or at the dinner table. She finds happiness in setting and arranging the dining table and preparing it for dinner.

It was routine for Dawn to go out with us to walk for a thousand steps, and Dawn loved such a routine of a few minute's walk after dinner. It was routine to talk about some elements of nature, like the moon and stars, trees, and chirping birds during such a walk.

Dawn is precisely good at following certain daily routines. She cleans her hands, washes her face thoroughly, and changes her clothes as soon as she returns from school and even after finishing virtual school. Thanks to Blaire, this even goes for brushing her teeth and washing her mouth systematically after every meal.

Dawn has an extraordinary talent for repeating and replaying dialogue and conversations, putting herself replacing a prime character. She can perform flawless mimicry, a literary composition, or parody in verse or prose. She does it all alone, without others' input or help.

Whenever she is in the mood, she goes to some nearby room area, leaving the family room to avoid other family members observing her activities of playing parody. But her performing parody is loud enough that one can listen if he wants to.

Initially, we watched and listened to her imitate her mom talking with her; of course, Dawn parodied Blaire in her absence. Conversations were routinely occurring between her and her mom, and we could understand those imitating perfectly.

After that, Dawn started imitating others whenever we went to family gatherings and parties. She focuses on her preferred guest and hosting parents to catch and grab conversations between hosting parents and their children. In most of those conversations, she saw mothers counseling their children on the proper etiquette and behaviors. Once we returned home, we observed her imitating the visited family, maybe on the same day or after a couple of days.

Similarly, she performs a parody of her favorite teacher's way of teaching and mixes the teacher's instructions on dos and don'ts to make it a perfect parody.

It is incredible to watch her single-handedly performing parody replacing different persons using low and high tone frequencies with proper gestures and actions close to perfection. She beautifully mixes emotions and dialogue and further supports with words like thanks, appreciated, and even sorry to perform correctly. She brilliantly captures a sequence of conversations. She repeats those depending on her mood.

She parodies all such activities while strolling within the home, in a separate area where family members are not watching her. She prefers to be in a less-illuminated place to recollect episodes and conversations with minute details and continue her passion while taking a leisurely walk. The preference for soft illumination may be to remain focused so no one can disturb her.

Dawn is a shy girl who does not like to talk with strangers, but once she gets the confidence, she becomes friendly. She is very talkative, and she talks using the correct words. She loves to speak once she gets acquainted.

Parents need to be careful and selective about their talk and behavior with such passions, even for watching TV shows and films, and many more. Like Dawn, children may register so casually that one may not notice them capturing those details.

It is needless to mention that parents and elders should follow basic protocols and etiquette, sacrificing their right to live life with freedom, considering their obligatory responsibility toward their children.

Every child is a masterpiece. Understanding a child's likes and dislikes, behavioral reactions and responses, and capacities and capabilities are required. Children consider their parents' role models and observe their parents keenly during their developmental age.

Human life comes with remarkable, unbelievable, mind-boggling powers. Unfortunately, a significant portion remains untapped for every individual. A child with congenital disabilities also comes with tremendous inbuilt energy, and we need to initiate and develop those to enable that child to live independently.

A naturally distinctive child tries to balance shortcomings by developing special inquisitive skills. Alternatively, sometimes they jumpstart to produce their earmarked talent, performances with some natural gift.

While discussing and recalling all the above, Blaire and Christine became so happy that they did not even feel sad and recognized it as the terrible phase we all had passed through successfully by the grace of God. It was a blessing in disguise; otherwise, it could have been more painful and severe.

We realized that children with congenital deformities and disabilities arrive intending to offer an opportunity to be humane, have countless life values, and establish a beautiful, lovely family and community filled with human values. It depends on how one would like to take on the challenges.

We concluded with the observation that children like Dawn are not commonly placed persons in this world; however, they come by taking birth to some families routinely. Their taking birth can be a part of the natural system, a self-governing, self-operating balancing system discussed in context with the subject. It is the natural balancing system of humanity, the human values amongst human beings.

These children come so naturally that some people take them casually and make mistakes in recognizing them. They visit with specially designed and assigned jobs as distinguished onlookers, distinctive observers, and witnesses to balance humanity within the family, society, and the community of human beings. If we look with a bit of wisdom and broad thinking, we will find a win-win situation. It is not the only way to transform and establish a beautiful world filled with caring persons; however, it can be one of the excellent ways.

"Looking at Dawn's innocence and cheerfulness," I concluded, "I always feel good and express gratification to God for gifting her into the family."

With all such discussions, today, we have a beautiful grown-up girl, and everyone has become emotional. I had preferred to get up to lean on the writing desk to relax, although connected with memories. I closed my eyes to visualize those days when Dawn had arrived through a long, painful journey to the family. It was all emotional and sentimental.

I appreciated Dawn's presence which offered parents and family ample opportunities to refine into loving, caring, compassionate persons and understand the wonderful world and its charismatic, self-governing operating systems.

I reviewed the entire film *Dawn Recalls* and enjoyed the complete sequence on my desk, the personal theater, and the probe into the past.

04

Perturbed Disheartened Blaire
Incredulous at Unforeseen Event

Blaire, the anxious mother of the newly born baby, huddled at the corner of a couch in the waiting lounge of a neonatal intensive child care unit. It was a morning session, and the waiting lounge was busy.

Christine and I, the grandparents of the newly born baby, had a place to sit on another couch.

A phone buzzed, and Blaire hurriedly got up to answer. She was so desperate that before the person on the other end started to communicate, she impatiently asked, "Hope everything is fine with my baby!"

After listening to the caller, she blurted out, "What is wrong with her baby's eyes?" She controlled her emotions and listened carefully to her raised queries about the health issues of her baby.

Assuming some severe problem, we also got up with the intent to support her, but we preferred to listen and be quiet, standing nearby to catch some clues about Dawn's health.

We purposefully did not face Blaire, as she might become emotional in our presence and get distracted while discussing critical issues.

We heard her say, "Are you sure?"

We could see that she was entirely shocked and dumbfounded as she helplessly asked for reconfirmation. Then she fearfully asked, "Does that mean some more syndromes may crop up as the baby grows?"

With each question, there was a briefing from the other end. Looking at Blaire anxiously listening to the briefing, we saw her nearly surrender to the unexpected worrying situation, and then we heard her saying, "Oh no."

She hung up the phone and appeared entirely dazed and forsaken. She tensely crashed on the couch again, murmuring, "Why me? Why does this have to happen to my baby?"

Her body was quivering, and she wanted to convey something to us, but her jaws were too clenched to utter a word. She closed her eyes to hide her melancholy, but the tears found ways to come out into the sudden shadowing silence.

We instantly suspected distressing information about Dawn, the newly born baby, our granddaughter.

However, we avoided rushing to Blaire and questioning her, although we had formulated enough understanding from the phone message and Blaire's body language. It was a spine-chilling moment, looking at Blaire's woes and misery and, at the same time, being the grandpa of a newly arrived baby.

Realizing how serious the situation was, we gave her some moments to overcome her grief and took our seats.

Nevertheless, Christine could not bear it.

She was sitting next to Blaire, anxiously watching the scene. Still, she did not rush to Blaire, as we had decided not to. She hinted to me that there must be something amiss. However, I managed the situation as deftly as possible by saying, "Please, it is not the time to think negatively and ask questions to Blaire."

I told her she could hug Blaire, her daughter, and calm her down but make sure not to question Blaire about the conversation.

Christine was upset and disappointed. She tried to determine if I had picked up any clues. She got up, a little unsteady, and wanted to understand the extent of the seriousness of Dawn's health issues before turning to her daughter.

Christine could not stand to see her daughter suffering. She wanted to provide moral support to soothe, console, and care for her daughter. She had many questions and anxieties, and that felt panicky to her.

She turned and bent down, supporting herself on my knees so that we could speak quietly, one-to-one, about her granddaughter's health issues (for which we were yet to have confirmed information) before she wanted to ask her daughter, but then she crashed to her knees with the stressful condition.

Fortunately, I had anticipated the situation and could support her and said, "Please, do not lose self-confidence or strength and be disheartened."

She wanted to be with her discouraged daughter to support her. Blaire was bawling, maybe looking for a shoulder to cry on and a way to release from her anguish. "Blaire needs you, your support, and you cannot break down," I said,

She was so distressed that before turning toward her daughter, she again turned and wanted strong backing and a feeling of solace from me. She asked, "Jay, what do you feel about Dawn?"

At the same time, Blaire could see we were struggling with stress and anxiety. She welcomed her mom to come to sit beside her.

Christine was offered more space on the couch by a lady sitting next to Blaire, and within a few moments, they understood each other's concerns. Moreover, they managed to calm down, giving confidence to each other. They must have realized that it was not the time to break down but to think about what could happen next and what they needed to do to resolve any issues.

Blaire managed to come out of her agony, and Christine also controlled her emotions. Both appeared hoisted, and that was a moment of relaxation.

Looking at the scene of Blaire and Christine comforting each other, I also got up to comfort them and point out that Dawn would need them more than ever under the prevailing predicted crucial situation, whatever it was.

Since Blaire had gathered some information, I wanted to know and comprehend Dawn's health issues and condition. Moreover, I wanted an opportunity to understand what issues Dawn was born with or what went wrong after birth that caused her to develop severe health problems.

We had seen Dawn was looking healthy after her arrival, and there had been no unpleasant information from a doctor or any nurse that gave us reason to worry. However, at this time, we preferred to remain silent.

Dawn was delivered traditionally and safely through the birth canal, and her birth was without any medical intervention. She was healthy-looking and beautiful, weighing almost seven pounds.

Blaire and Ryan were happy being parents, and seeing them excited and pleased and being grandparents, traditionally called Nana and Nani, increased our happiness at seeing the newborn baby.

On the day of Dawn's arrival, the hospital staff was bustling. Maybe there had been inundated expectant mothers and deliveries on that particular day. No matter how busy, it was essential to avoid crowding in the corridor near the guest viewing window of the newborn babies' care center.

Dawn was transferred to the NICU soon after birth due to mild meconium aspiration and routine health-related checkups. We all had thought it might be a matter of a few hours or a day or two. It was anticipated and taken for granted that everything was in a manageable state.

Some close friends and family members were with us. We had amicably decided to wait for an invitation or signal from the nurse to meet the baby. Although we stayed in expectation, the nurse did not signal, and the baby remained asleep. We could observe that her sleep was a little restless, with some breathing medical devices fixed on her as if something was disturbing her or making her breathless and uncomfortable.

The excitement of the close friends and family members was evident as they kept trying to find a spot at the glass window to steal beautiful moments looking at her. We all were also eagerly waiting to see a glance of a lovely smile on the baby's face. We wanted to look into her eyes to welcome her and express gratitude for her arrival.

The hospital staff had routinely informed Blaire about the probability of being discharged the next day as there were no significant issues in delivering the baby, the healthy condition of the mother, and the expected fast recovery from mild meconium aspiration.

However, we were stressed and tense, looking at the new baby's non-responsiveness and apparent look. Being non-medical field persons, we could not understand the meconium aspiration and related health issues of the baby. We had no alternative but to console each other and ask irrelevant questions to get indirect soothing effects.

Christine repeatedly asked, "Jay, what do you feel about Dawn?" Moreover, I had no alternative but to comfort her in the non-availability of medical reports.

"Do not worry," I replied and said, "Nothing major seems wrong with the baby; otherwise, doctors would have gone for some more vigorous medical tests and examinations."

Christine had an opportunity to be a grandma and could visit the baby for a glance. However, we remained worried, and she kept showing her concern by asking questions in different forms. She suspected some problems with Dawn. A newborn not opening her eyes, not responding to any calls, and sleeping almost unconscious made Christine worry about serious issues.

The hospital management proposed the couple celebrate the perfect day of becoming parents. It offered a candlelit dinner in the hospital room, following their management routine and anticipating that everything was well. The hospital staff greeted Blaire and Ryan with a glass of wine.

Nevertheless, Blaire remained nervous and distressed at the dinner table. The baby was under intensive care with multiple medical devices to clear meconium from her trachea and stomach, and Blaire did not disturb the innocent baby.

They did not enjoy the candlelit-dinner celebration. Blaire remained in a predicament throughout the dinner, as being a mother could not be able to interact with Dawn so far. Nevertheless, as per the report from the medical staff, the baby was recovering fast, and she would be fine as soon as possible. After dinner, Ryan had to leave the hospital dejectedly late at night.

05

Concerns and Sleepless Night
Apprehensive Christine and Jay

Blaire had a sleepless night as she kept visiting the neonatal intensive care unit to steal a moment to look at Dawn. She wanted to warmly welcome her daughter into their lives and express her love and gratitude.

She had asked the nurse to inform her when the baby was ready to interact. The night was full of concerns and apprehensions for her.

We were at home and could not sleep due to the many ambiguities and anxieties with suddenly raised unforeseen circumstances. Christine was perplexed and kept raising different questions, and I tried to answer and explain in different ways based on my understanding, assumptions, and hypotheses.

We remained worried throughout the night about Blaire's woes and miseries and our granddaughter Dawn's health issues.

During resting, I felt a heaviness in my chest. I could not sleep and wanted to remain diverted to vent out stressful conditions. I have preexisting cardiac issues and had recently undergone bypass surgery, making it a little risky and unsafe to stay stressed and anxious.

Christine, I know my daughter, Blaire, is powerful, but I have seen her for the first time desperately breaking down."

When Christine came out with an unanswerable question, "If Dawn has some severe health issues, do you feel those would be curable?"

With all the opacities in the absence of concluding reports from the concerned doctors, she wanted to give herself some relief and the feeling of taking over her worries to feel a little relaxed. It was usual in our life to talk it out and then indulge in extended spiritual thinking, maybe to divert the discussion and feel some relief.

Christine knows me as a strong person who would not easily break down and dishearten by problems. She wanted some reaffirmation that could comfort her.

"Do not worry," I said. "Trust in God, and we can always register petition with prayers for blessings and God's grace."

"Blaire is a strong lady who can manage any eventualities confidently and succeed. We have two sons who can rush to assist if needed, and they can all join as a team to do their best for our lovely Dawn if crises arise."

I added, "Both brothers of Blaire can always reach out to her in the worst situations to support, share, and bring her out from her woes and miseries."

Christine was sporadically becoming downhearted, so I continued with communication to keep her engaged. I knew that if I blended my conversation with some spiritual talk, she would immediately get hooked up, so I started with a more elaborate explanation.

"Do you remember the day when Blaire informed us that she was pregnant, and we all celebrated?" I began. "We had also casually discussed with Blaire that there was a starting point of bringing a new life into the world of human beings, and God had selected her as a medium. In other words, almighty God has blessed, trusted, and empowered Blaire to remain as an intermediate, a mediator. Moreover, she remained proud and elevated to deliver a baby."

To stay busy and divert from nervousness, we talked and discussed many more subjects elaborately that night, connecting prevailing situations with Dawn and Blaire. Christine was getting engrossed, as she had enjoyed pregnancy three times.

I continued, "The fetus remains united and involved deeply with the mother through the placenta, the umbilical cord, the natural lifeline support system to continue growing, surviving, and developing biological features. The pregnancy keeps the mother fascinated and captivated until she delivers a baby. Blaire remained gratified with the charismatic event of being a mother, and that experience can happen in any woman's life."

Christine said, "I know very well that a woman becomes different when pregnant. I have also seen how Blaire has changed with pregnancy."

"The baby within her womb feels relaxed, safe, and secure and remains carefree, calm, and happy under the lovely caring shelter of a mother." She had also noticed that Blaire, with her pregnancy, had become more lovely and caring.

Continuing our talk, we experienced Blaire transforming into a lovely, compassionate lady. During pregnancy, she got an opportunity to grow into her role as a mother to redefine herself and enhance her superb qualities through fine-tuning by associating with a most innocent form of a human being, getting shaped within her womb.

"The baby remains utterly dependent on the mother for almost nine months, the gestation period," I pointed out. "Blaire must have communicated assurances to her baby, the fetus, throughout the pregnancy."

Through all such discussions, Christine remembered her pregnancies. She wanted to divert her mind, so she asked with inquisitiveness and curiosity, "Does the baby communicate with the mother during pregnancy? Moreover, she said, "She had also experienced intimate participation with a baby in her womb, a platonic relationship, and had enjoyed those beautiful moments. However, what do you think, Jay?"

"A pregnant lady talks to her baby frequently and for such a lengthy duration of pregnancy when it appears to be one-sided communication? Mother and baby become empowered and made competent by waking up and perceiving each other during the pregnancy to remain in direct contact and stay involved effectively."

I continued, "There must be an implied accord, concurrence, and understanding between the mother and fetus for their shared, joint actions. Both must perform admirably and persistently during pregnancy to care for and love each other before birth. Thereby, they can remain happy and gratified with each other.

Through an implied agreement, it is an assurance by the mother to perform abidingly and support her child under any and every happy or sad instance, event, episode, and situation. Moreover, the association should continue even after birth until the child attains maturity and gains the ability to live independently.

In other words, it is the process of implicit concurrence, to cooperate and coordinate with intimate harmony, and to perform persistently with each other during different stages of pregnancy and subsequently giving birth, and after that, until the child attains maturity."

While discussing all general topics, I saw an opening to talk about Dawn.

"Nobody knew what was going wrong with Dawn," I said to Christine. "Presume Dawn was born with congenital anomalies or has developed health issues after birth. In any case, the immediate family members should share the responsibilities with Blaire. Furthermore, we should be available to Blaire, prioritizing any of her and Dawn's issues and emergencies."

I intended to extend the talk until we got tired enough to sleep. I explained to Christine, "Most mothers undergo a caesarian procedure where the doctor snips the placenta to disconnect the baby from the mother. It is a lifeline that a baby has enjoyed for an extended nine months of pregnancy, remaining carefree and solely dependent. Momentarily, the baby comes under sudden shock and feels deserted."

"It is the most extended phase of life in human beings to be physically sluggish and lethargic even though having a complete body with the life force, the ensoulment, spirit. Isn't it wonderful that the baby cries to jumpstart her systems to live self-sustained lives even after getting disconnected from the mother? After the birth, the baby starts looking around, maybe searching for the mother to express gratitude for supporting the transient phase to land her into this beautiful world and convey that she is fine and not to worry."

Then I had to appease and pacify Christine by saying, "Any mother would not like to remember the terrible pain she endures while giving birth to her baby. The instance of delivering a baby is to share responsibility with God by becoming a medium to bring a new human life to this world. And that becomes a big celebration for a woman to be a mother."

"In this case, Blaire would also like to feel relaxed and happy after successfully giving birth to her child," said Christine. "However, to our misfortune, we could not see Blaire enjoying such moments."

It was a tense and crying situation.

"Every mother wishes that her baby will remain happy and go through minimal suffering during her entire life," I said, "Likewise, Blaire must have thought so too."

"The mother also becomes empowered once she successfully delivers the baby," Christine participated.

"At the same time," I added, "Blaire can live comfortably, contented, and maintain her happiness and confidence with minimal suffering. Any mother gets filled with extra strength from within as she wants to connect, care for, and love her baby, but Blaire did not have a chance."

Being parents, we remained anxious, caressed,

"Blaire could not rest even for a while after giving birth to her baby," Christine reflected. "She must be feeling tired and terrible under the circumstances."

I concluded, "She remains sustained to do her best to love and care for the newcomer in her life."

06

Cherished Motherhood
Unwavering, Steadfast Routines

"If Dawn is diagnosed with severe anomalies, how will Blaire handle her?" Christine anxiously asked.

I did not think we should have such negative thoughts without any information about the medical reports by the concerned children's hospital authorities. However, since Christine had the question in her mind, I thought to appease her. I said, "Blaire is competent but emotional and caring, and she would understand her responsibility toward her baby. Moreover, she would make every crucial decision to protect her baby, if required in life."

"I wish Blaire would accept the reality. Dawn may be diagnosed with congenital anomalies."

I continued, "She will also not hesitate to get support services from different sources. Dawn will get the best treatments and training through experienced visiting trainers and therapists in consultation with medical practitioners to make Dawn independent."

"I can see solid confidence in Blaire and readiness to dedicate her life happily, at the same time, without feeling abandoned for her personal life, if such misfortune comes to her as her destiny. She will completely get involved and remain committed to her daughter. If required, she can take over as a key therapist and do all sorts of therapies determinedly and untiringly."

I confidently comforted Christine and said, "Blaire would do her best so that Dawn enjoys this wonderful world happily. Being a mother, she would also make sure that Dawn would go through minimal suffering during her life. At the same time, she would ensure that to live comfortably and happily, having the steadfast support of her parents."

All such conversations were based on intricacy, guessing, and probabilities of the situation as and when it arose; however, Christine remained low and perplexed.

At almost midnight, I decided to finish with a beautiful anecdote, and I continued, "Nicodemus was Pharisee and a very wealthy person. He had liked Jesus and wanted to attend the congregation but was always afraid for some reason, so he secretly met Jesus many times.

"Once, Nicodemus approached a congregation where Lord Jesus was preaching a sermon, addressing a gathering of His disciples, and he asked Jesus when he could see the Supreme God. And Jesus had answered, 'Once you become a Child.'

"Nicodemus could not understand and reply that he had already passed through his childhood and become a fully grown person; did that mean he had lost the opportunity to see and meet the Supreme God?"

"Jesus replied, 'No, Nicodemus. Becoming a child means being innocent, pure, serene, sacred, full of love, care, and kindness, and being a righteous person.'

With that, Lord Jesus opened the doorways of dawn for him and all others who wanted to understand the Supreme God.

"God did not send Him to condemn and judge the world, but rather to save the world and its people from their sin."

Christine grabbed what she wanted.

To remain connected with Blaire, Dawn's subjects, and keep up Christine's interest, I solaced, "Do not worry. We need not worry and remain in any dilemma. Blaire will do the most required for her daughter. She will take care of and perform all her requisite duties and prove herself a lovely, responsible mother. Furthermore, we will ~~also~~ remain available to support Blaire in completing her commitments."

We continued further and discussed how the fertilized egg, the embryo, develops once the pregnancy is confirmed, passing through tremendous mystical changes and charismatic transformations. The fetus's body form gradually reaches a stage of ensoulment, the process of spiriting the body, and after that, it can be considered a baby human being.

As per theology, ensoulment is when a rational person gains a soul. The fetus grows systematically and steadily inside the uterus as per the programming of genes until the pregnancy ends with labor pains and birth. The fetus grows as a complete human being in a cuddle position. The curled-up situation feels secure until the baby emerges through birth.

Even though all organs and systems have developed, the fetus remains entirely dependent on the mother through the umbilical cord to survive during pregnancy. All activities for survival, like breathing, eating, excreting, and growing, including flowing blood into the fetus, is from the mother through the placenta. The baby need not worry about anything until she remains in the mother's womb, the coziest shelter.

The statement does not challenge medical science and expert professionals' knowledge and is only relevant to the subject. A physically inactive means the fetus has developed different parts with all vital body organs but remains dependent on the mother's systems for all essential activities. It is the most extended phase of human life, as inactive before birth.

The derived presumption is that along with brain development, a collective unconscious mind also develops in a fetus during gestation, with memories collected from previous generations. It is the loveliest experience of life for the fetus. It is a state of just being, to be present. In other words, it may not be exaggerating to say a form of a tranquil place to be within oneself, which is the gestation period.

After enjoying a carefree, peaceful, effortless life within the mother's womb, one might not have a chance to experience the same comfort and peace after birth during the entire life. Consequently, it is pretty evident one might remain to search and keep looking for peace and harmony, but the thirst never quenches.

Those memories cannot be retrieved, as they have gone into the collective unconscious mind. However, one tends to look for such a happy, blissful life through personification and archetypes models in symbolic form throughout life.

One must become increasingly aware of the wisdom available in one's personal and collective unconscious and learn to live in harmony. It consists of prototypes and primary images to achieve peace, unity, and completeness. The best examples of the collective unconscious model include the parent-child relationship, especially between mother and child. We remember such forms and dreams and try to fix and interpret wisdom from time to time.

The world has everything for everyone. People may not know what thoughts and images are in their collective unconscious but then presume that the spirit, a soul, can be tapped into the collective unconscious in a crisis. The search will continue until the world symbolically resembles a mother's womb, meaning a lovely, caring, and compassionate world. Consequently, the world's people will have minimum worries, apprehensions, and unhappiness."

We discussed the possibilities of connecting with differently-abled children, as they also appear carefree and remain happy while being in their world. The objective (unbiased) psyche (spirit, soul) is distinct from the personal unconscious. The personal unconscious arises from the worldly experiences of the individual.

These humans are typically responsible for deep-seated beliefs and instincts, such as spirituality and religiosity. The inherent instinct, the instinctive desire that the world becomes like a mother's womb, the shelter for every human being, may be symbolic imaginary memories of the collective unconscious. Ultimately, it is to achieve a mutual agreement with existence and to feel completeness.

Every person inherits a collective unconscious mind, which is the center of imagining salvation. Inevitably, every such person wants to attain symbolic places like heaven, swarga, nirvana, paradise, and many more as per their beliefs. All have imagined these salvation places where one can go after death as a place for eternal peace and happiness. One can return to a similar home, a realm of Almighty God the Father, Allah, or Paramatma, which has lasting peace and blissfulness that everyone enjoys a little bit of it, a glance of it before birth during the gestation period.

People must become increasingly aware of the wisdom available in their personal and collective unconscious and learn to live in harmony having contentment. The collective unconscious consists of archetypes (models) or ancient religious images under spirituality to achieve unity and totality. We remember such archetypes and dreams and try to fix and interpret their wisdom from time to time.

The fetus and mother have a direct connection through the umbilical cord, and every aspect of the fetus's life depends on the mother's mental and physical health. When the fetus; comes under deep despair and suffering during pregnancy, the mother may participate and vice versa. Sometimes the pregnant woman also goes through archetype dreams during deep sleep. Alternatively, as discussed under the implied concurrence hypothesis, it may happen as the promise to take care of and coordinate each other's feelings and sentiments.

The derivatives and assumptions explain that children born with congenital anomalies have hidden power as observers and as a part of a natural self-governing balancing system for lovely, caring, compassionate life connections as per hypotheses.

We can hypothesize the unconscious mind is an iceberg.[1] A portion above the water represents the conscious mind, while everything below can be illustrated as unconscious.

A significant portion of the iceberg is underwater, and most of the time, we ignore the massive part of the iceberg which not seen. It leads us to consider that awareness of the human brain is insufficient, while an unaware part of our brain is enormous.

The effects of unconscious feelings can lead to difficulties in social interactions, obsessive uncontrollable behaviors, related issues, and more considerations of irrational behaviors of children born with congenital anomalies. These are not yet proven and can be inspiring to come out evidentially.

However, relate such assumptions in context with children born with congenital anomalies. After all, the human mind cannot remain dumped because some

---

1. Kendra Cherry, "What Is the Subconscious?" Very Well Mind, https://www.verywellmind.com/what-is-the-unconscious-2796004

genetic malfunction has occurred, and the brain has not developed to show specific, typical characteristics.

Doctors would test and examine shortcomings as medical science researches with the standards of a typical child, but it does not end there. There can be many more unknown, unexplored characteristics that may or may not remain altered and damaged. The brain of a child born with congenital anomalies (differently-abled child) may work simply as a receptor, without scrutinizing information, and keep working to pass on observations to a self-governing natural balancing system for humanity.

People live with many probabilities and beliefs, followed by faith followers, atheists, and monotheists. Everyone has a reason to pursue their ideas. The purpose is to open up one more convincing and possible doorway or device, which may be under the discussed hypothesis. The aim is to promote human life values like love, care, and compassion within human communities.

Parents need not think as unfortunate having such a child born in the family but develop positive aspects and take care, gain an incentive for upliftment, and remain motivated to be loving, caring, compassionate persons.

Furthermore, as discussed, many more persons already on the team have reasons to continue and remain involved, which may create chain reactions that can help balance humankind in the people of this world.

Thus, as assumed, children born with congenital anomalies or acquired life-threatening diseases after birth have their connection with the natural self-governing balancing system to establish love, care, and compassion. Human communities' life values are all-time requirements, and these children are one of the routes to achieve those.

Compassion is a prerequisite for the establishment of humanity in this world. Compassion is not a relationship between the caretaker and the sufferer; compassion is deeply rooted in human awareness.

We need to harness community builders. Unless someone proves the contrary, the assumptions can yield much more in human communities and have valid reasons and arguments. Connections to believe and give comfort to every concerned and associated person.

Carl Gustav Jung, born on July 26, 1875, was a psychiatrist who founded analytical psychology in response to Sigmund Freud's psychoanalysis. Jung proposed and developed extroverted and introverted personalities, models, and collective unconsciousness concepts.[2] His work and study have remained influential in the study of religion, literature, and related fields. He believed

---

2 https://www.google.com/search?q=how+many+years+old+jung+collective+unconscious+read+theory&rlz=1C1CHZN enUS957US957&oq=&aqs=chrome.0.69i59i45012.15475262j0j15&sourceid=chrome&ie=UTF-8
https://www.britannica.com/biography/Carl-Jung/Character-of-his-psychotherapy -
https://www.verywellmind.com/what-is-the-unconscious-2796004 -Views are medically reviewed by Ami Morin, a psychotherapist, and mental health trainer, and updated by Kendra Cherry.

human beings remain connected through their ancestors' shared experiences. The collective unconscious is to give meaning to the world. His work of 1902 differentiated two types of personalities, introverted (in-ward looking) and extroverted (Outward looking).

Dawn shifted to the neonatal intensive childcare unit of a specialized children's hospital for twenty-one long days of close observation. We had nothing more to do except keep worrying and thinking about Dawn. What would happen?

Christine asked Blaire, "What if Dawn comes out with some other deformities and her vision and hearing impairments?"

Initially, it appeared absurd, the misplaced question to Blaire, like scratching the wound, but then I could observe that Blaire happily accepted the conversation with Christine. It was a perfect moment, and I saw Blaire wanted something to talk about to distract her from routine hospital scenes.

Blaire told Christine, "Congenital anomalies can develop during pregnancy. However, most occur during the first trimester, when the baby's organs start forming. They can also develop during the later phase of pregnancy when the organs grow."

"With advanced medical science and technology, the mother knows that a child is developing with lifelong, enduring anomalies and other related syndromes, but termination of pregnancy after the sixteenth to twentieth weeks will be risky. A mother may have to make a hard decision to discontinue the pregnancy."

Blaire was becoming nervous, but then she continued.

"After birth, until the child develops hues vision, gradation or identifying a variety of color, the child uses other senses to perceive and identify objects and persons. Shades vision imaging can play a significant role in developing the required intelligence for responses and reactions.

"After birth, the child is considered an innocent and sacred being for the initial period. The child uses senses of vision, touch, and smell limited to feeding. However, the child needs to be independent to survive by using insights and intelligence to interact with people, including the parents. It means that the child starts using the conscious mind by having experienced worldly connections and affairs."

To divert from the topic during our conversation, imagining the worst that could happen for Dawn, I had to take over and start with an entirely different subject. I said, "You knew that a child born with clenched palms and feet inherited ancestral traits that indicate an independent survival mode to have safety and security?

"However, the clenched limbs are also a symbolic pattern presumed for the ensoulment of the fetus, arriving through sneaky, clandestine (secret) strings. The fetus's soul and spirit may land from outside, somewhere else during pregnancy. We can understand further through the belief of silver string, the cord, and soul parting from the body."

The ensoulment of the fetus is a miraculous incident for every life on the planet. Human beings are highly evolved lives, and mothers are fortunate and empowered to become a medium to have such opportunities.

07

Blaire Comes Under Trepidation
Family Members Unite to Comfort Blaire

Blaire entered the neonatal intensive childcare unit with prayers and confidence that her baby would be fine and she would be happy to welcome her daughter into their lives. It was early morning, the very next day of Dawn's birth.

Christine and Jay had an opportunity to glance through the viewing window after her birth and found a healthy-looking baby but then transferred to the neonatal intensive care unit for health issues.

Blaire met a nurse in the corridor who accompanied her to the baby's cradle. Blaire was very anxious, as she had no opportunity to make skin-to-skin contact with or even feed her baby, and she hoped that Dawn would be fine. She wanted to interact with her baby for the first time and to express her gratitude.

The nurse informed Blaire that the baby was primarily cleared from meconium and now breathing comfortably. "Good luck," she uttered before getting busy with the other babies.

Blaire wanted to feel her baby and get satisfaction from being a mother. She also wanted to thoroughly examine her baby's entire body to get confirmation and feel comfortable. When Blaire touched her baby for the first time, it was natural for her to feel good. The baby struggled to open her eyes with her mother's touch, and unfortunately, Blaire noticed a white dot with cloudy eyes.

She immediately anticipated severe issues, and her happiness turned into fear and concern to find the answer for the dot and cloudy eyes, a spot on the cornea. Blaire was also concerned about Dawn's sluggishness. She immediately rushed to the nurse, shared her observation, expressed her apprehension, and requested to speak with the doctor in charge as soon as possible.

Dawn was born with meconium aspiration and had difficulty in breathing; however, hospital staff shifted her to the childcare department to primarily resolve her breathing issue. Unfortunately, it was a busy day for the hospital staff; maybe more pregnant women had visited than scheduled and expected. The nursing staff might have thought to complete the thorough routine health checkups as soon as they complete life-threatening emergency cases and get the time slot out of their busyness. Dawn weighed seven pounds and was a healthy-looking baby at birth. The issue of meconium aspiration was detected and solved to breathe comfortably.

The priority was to clear the meconium for the medical staff and see that the baby started breathing. Removing the meconium from the baby's respiratory tracts, food canal, and stomach was essential. The baby must survive to avoid complications, including severe respiratory infections.

The panicky nursing staff and doctors' movements made Blaire more nervous. Being a paramedical professional, she preferred to be quiet and allow them to look into the issue.

The in-charged medical staff assured and comforted Blaire to be enduring and keep patient, as they would immediately take all due action. They decided to transfer the baby to a specialized children's hospital, considering the other severe conditions in their observation. Immediately, they shifted the baby to an ophthalmology checking room to complete preliminary eye exams.

With all said and done, Blaire lost her patience and asked, "Is it serious? I am nervous and worried."

"Sorry, we cannot say anything at this time," she got the answer. "Please keep the faith and hope nothing serious comes up. We will inform you as soon as the tests are over and the doctor concludes."

The hospital staff opted not to conclude anything before the specialized doctor checked and created concluding reports.

Looking at the suddenly developing scene, the anxious mother dejectedly returned to the waiting lounge and leaned on her mother's shoulder. She expressed her gloom and sadness about the white spots in Dawn's cloudy eyes and crossed her fingers against our anxious inquiries and questions.

I had preferred not to inquire further.

After some time, the nurse informed us that the doctor had confirmed white dots and cloudy eyes due to congenital deformities in her eyes. However, they would not like to say anything more until the concerned specialist pays a visit to examine the baby to conclude the report.

We realized that the baby might get vision issues. We became anxious, nervous, and panicky. Nevertheless, we preferred to be supportive by calming down tense situations rather than discussing the probable severity of issues.

We had no alternative but to strengthen the willpower of our daughter, Blaire. We hugged Blaire and said, "Look, we both, grandparents of your baby, are here with you, and you being the mother of the baby, have to build up confidence."

We encouraged her to accept challenges. Furthermore, we blessed her and gave our assurances to support her.

She was getting loaded with stress and tension, thinking that if some more severe deformities were detected and declared, which might be lifelong, then what? How would she keep up to continue with inspiration for the rest of her baby's life?

Meanwhile, she noticed us with geared-up confidence and attitudes to face the situation and yield the best out of the prevailing conditions. In response, she built up her faith to deal with the situation.

To our surprise, we found that she also got charged to meet what might come, and we could see in her the resolution and commitment to do the best for her baby. She expressed that she has geared up to face anything worse than possible. She would do her best from her side and was confident of achieving the best with our support.

Now she was no longer a frantic mother, as she had come out from her disappointment, shock, and anxiety. Ryan, her husband, also rushed to the hospital, knowing the developed issues. We spoke to our sons, who lived in New Jersey and Florida, to inform them about the current situation. We pushed Blaire to discuss Dawn's health issues with her brothers to lessen her gloomy dejection and to remain diverted.

She prepared herself to take necessary actions to find second medical professionals' opinions through her resources to understand her daughter's likely problems and severities. During such predicament, we received a phone call from our eldest son,

"Hi, Dad,"

"We both brothers knew the probabilities of Dawn's health, and rest assured, we will be there to support you. Don't worry. Please take care of your health and everyone, including Blaire. Hopefully, Blaire will receive the necessary doctor reports as soon as possible to take suitable actions in the right direction. Please keep us posted with updates."

Dawn was already in the emergency neonatal intensive care unit - NICU under observation. She needed to transfer to the specialized children's hospital. Blaire was already discharged from the maternity hospital as scheduled.

Blaire was worried about me as I had severe heart attacks and had bypass surgery the previous year. With her current dicey situation, she never wanted her backup support to be paralyzed or fail with such panic. We were getting upset and aching over her circumstances, but she gave us solace and assured us that she would manage this predicament.

She convinced us to go home and rest, as we had not slept the previous night and remained anxious. We were satisfied seeing her as a geared-up mother ready to perform the best for her child.

We left for home, and Blaire remained busy with her brothers, who had rushed to assist their sister. They used their best browsing skills to find resources on the internet and kept feeding additional information to

Blaire. She provided them with medical terminology to understand Dawn's problem and do proper web searches. Both brothers supported Blaire in finding the best ophthalmologists, surgeons, medical professionals, and hospitals, as surgery was inevitable.

The children's hospital had decided to keep Dawn under close observation and thorough investigation to find any other issues she might develop during the initial days after the birth with such diagnoses. We all, including Blaire, had to leave the hospital, leaving the newly born baby, Dawn, in the hospital for three weeks, 21 long days as scheduled by doctors. At home, all remained worried about what might be wrong with such a healthy, beautiful baby. We kept praying to Almighty God to protect this child.

Before we received the final reports on Dawn's congenital anomalies, we struggled to understand which doctors and hospitals could come to our rescue in treating Dawn under the recommendation and consultation with hospital doctors. We needed to understand more details about the issues, emergencies, probabilities of repair, medical treatments, and surgery and to obtain an appointment. We wanted to provide the best possible treatment to Dawn to resolve the unexpected traumatic situation.

08

Predicament: Vision or Blindness
It could have been Worse

The concerned medical team kept Dawn under observation for almost three weeks in the specialized children's hospital. It was routine to be in the waiting lounge of the children's hospital from early morning till late evening to remain updated with any other issues Dawn might be developing.

A phone ring hummed.

Blaire, an anxious mother of the newly born baby, lifts the phone to respond. It was protocol; the concerned pediatrician wanted to make sure that she talked only to Blaire, the baby's mother. The doctor asked, "Hi, who is on the line? Am I speaking to Blaire about a newborn baby named Dawn?" And she abruptly responded, "Yes, I am."

"Is everything okay with her baby?"

The doctor despondently voiced, "No!"

A doctor explained, "After completing preliminary tests and examinations, we confirmed that Dawn has congenital anomalies. She has a vision issue, and you will receive a report soon. At present, she will not be able to see anything. She is almost like a blind child."

I was anxious to understand what could be wrong with Dawn. Has she developed any other deformities or disabilities during three weeks of hospitalization and close observation?

At the same time, I overheard some random words from the communication with Blaire that there can be some severe issues that may also develop, and those anomalies might put her into more chronic situations in her life.

Blaire, a disheartened, anxious mother, could not talk much, so she hung up the phone to finish her communication. It was an unforeseen episode for all of us.

Blaire cried in distress, saying, "Why did this happen to her?"

We understood the grieving situation and preferred not to react immediately to her despair until she calmed down and could come out.

As discussed, Christine wanted to comfort Blaire, who was nervously breaking down. She encouraged Blaire with rock-hard self-control and determination. By the grace of God, within a few moments, I could see that they understood each other's concerns and had managed to calm down, giving strength to each other.

Looking at Blaire and Christine comforting each other, I took the opportunity to reassure Blaire by saying to her, "Dawn will need us more than ever with the prevailing situation."

We wanted to understand which those severe issues would develop further.

Blaire controlled her emotion and decided to speak to the doctor to get more information. The doctor further reported that Dawn had syndromes under *Peter's anomaly* and would not be able to see unless the surgeon found surgery possible. Along with the blindness, there can be many more issues Dawn may show with her growing up under Peter's anomaly.

With such a medical report, we all had processed the news that Dawn was a blind child and, along with her blindness, she might develop other health issues. Blaire was shocked. She and Ryan were unhappy, as a child with such severe problems was not what they had thought of and dreamed.

Blaire was sobbing and bawling. It was the worst situation that we, as parents, had ever faced in our lives. Blaire was in heavy anguish for the first time in her life. We immediately realized that there was no other alternative but to console her.

After passing through this grieving condition, to our surprise, Blaire suddenly came out with a firm determination to do the best for her baby under the prevailing situation. We saw our daughter with a different personality as a medical professional.

She immediately managed herself and came out of the grief, which was like a boosting dose of encouragement to everyone. We got ready to think of what next, to come out with minimal damage to the newborn baby.

It was natural for Blaire and Ryan to feel disheartened and discouraged by the sudden arrival of a baby with congenital deformities, a distinctive child in their life. Instead of happily returning home with a baby from the hospital after her birth, they would have to visit Dawn in the specialized children's hospital for three weeks.

We had nothing more to do during the long 21 days of Dawn's hospitalization except routine visits with Blaire to see Dawn at the hospital. After completing a scheduled visit, we had to pass through the appalling phase of spending the rest of the day at home worrying and thinking about Blaire and her future with her baby.

After twenty-one days, Dawn would be at home, but she would not see her parents. She would not see her mother, and her mother would have to manage her blind baby. It was terrible to think about scenarios.

A couple of days before Dawn's birth, Christine and I had planned a short trip to our country of origin, India, and reached the airport to go. By the grace of God, we had intuition and got gut feelings that Blaire would need us, so we canceled our trip, withdrew our tickets at the Newark airport itself, and returned home.

Blaire was tired and discouraged from the routine of going back and forth from home to hospital to home, but then we assured her of our complete support.

Looking at the circumstances developed, we accepted the realities of life, confirming, "Whatever had to happen has already happened. Let us not break down and must keep visiting Dawn in the hospital with positivity."

Frank, the elder son, was fully informed about the situation and had searched for information in detail, coordinating with Andy. Blaire sent the medical doctor's report to her brothers to browse with a specific search engine on the internet. They had come up with more information about Peter's anomaly so Blaire could understand the symptoms and syndromes that might develop and the worst that could happen to Dawn.

Blaire also got encouragement to think further about what every one of us could do for Dawn. "It is not the time to think about why it had to happen with Dawn," I told her.

"Everyone should think and remain focused on what they can do so that Dawn can see her parents and the beautiful world. God must have decided something for Dawn and every one of us."

I encouraged Blaire by counseling her that pain and suffering come to the extent that one can bear and tolerate. We must join by becoming a team for the natural self-governing system for Dawn, the beautiful soul, and there might be some purpose for her arrival to the family. All must collectively put in our efforts, so Dawn gets the required treatments and remains blessed, so she gets the vision and enjoys her life should be our target now.

Blaire was cursing herself for giving such a life to her baby. I had to bring her out of that guilt, so I explained, "You being a paramedical practitioner, must have taken all due care during your pregnancy, so do not even think to feel guilty. Dawn's soul may feel uncomfortable if you curse yourselves."

Moreover, I added, "It was good that we returned from the airport, postponing our trip. Both your brothers' families are within the country, and we all can take the challenge of caring for Dawn. We assured each other to work jointly to share any severe unexpected problems that may pop up." They all had consoled Blaire, telling her it was not the time to get discouraged but to think about what best we should do for the baby, Dawn.

To lift everyone's mood, I said that we are in the world's most advanced country, where such a baby can be treated in the best possible ways and come out successfully with minimal damage. Everyone seconded their assurance that they would work, with full involvement, to resolve Dawn's health issues to the best possible extent.

Blaire had gained confidence and got boosted up. We could see her with an entirely changed mood and approach in looking at the prevailing circumstances. We could also see changes in her attitude towards prevailing circumstances to provide the best possible treatments for a newborn baby.

"Hey, Dad, do not worry about anything." She had decided to see how her child could come out with minimal health issues. We saw her getting busy contacting her resources and coordinating with Andy and Frank, her brothers.

Blaire was apprehensive about the newly developed situation after Dawn's birth, but she had appeased herself by looking at the steadfast support from family members. She remained boosted to schedule and plan all possible appointments as suggested through reports and after knowing the probabilities of issues from the concerned medical professionals.

We had also received phone calls from distant family members, friends, and relatives inquiring about Dawn's health and possible medical problems. We asked them to help us through prayers to God, so we could all support Blaire in finding the best resources to come out successfully from unforeseen events. I explicitly asked them to give me some time and told them I would call back as soon as we knew more about the health issues.

We never wanted Blaire to be emotional while speaking to different persons and diverge from the significant job of finding the best doctors, pediatric ophthalmologist surgeons, and hospitals. The surgery was inevitable within a particular time frame, and I took responsibility for answering those incoming phone calls.

To avoid increasing their anxieties, I had never reported to any friends and relatives about Dawn's medical report and its issues. I had a gut feeling that Dawn would be fine and decided to give everyone a straightforward, simple answer, saying, "The baby developed primary issues of meconium aspiration. However, the medical team has already addressed those issues, and Dawn will be fine within three to four weeks."

I continued to convey such information to well-wishers for a few weeks until incoming calls decreased significantly.

We had to bring Dawn, a blind child, into the home. The hospital discharged Dawn with a file containing various required examinations and test reports. As per the report, Dawn needed cornea transplantation to have some of her vision, but to what extent would it be known after successful cornea transplantation, provided no complications develop?

After desperately searching online, Andy found the name of Dr. Zee Herald at North Chester Hospital, a cornea specialist for children born with Peter's anomaly deformities which matched with recommendations from discharging hospital doctors. We all decided unanimously to visit him with Dawn. No appointment was available for three months, but Blaire used her good offices and got an early appointment.

The prime factor was to get a cornea donor within 90 to 120 days, preferably a child of a similar age. Besides, the transplanted cornea should remain uninfected for the initial few years.

As if this was not enough, Dawn had developed acute acid reflux problems and many more related issues of meconium aspiration. She used to have disturbed sleep and cried severely and heavily at night. We all had shared timings to manage her issues.

Unfortunately, we could not resolve the issue until we got the preliminary appointment with Dr. Zee Herald. We were in a dilemma. If Dawn's problems continued to such a date, how would we travel so long with her? How would Dr. Zee examine her eyes? The only solution we could find for that day was that Dawn needed to get exhausted by crying and become silent at the right time, which was a little cruel way to conclude.

Blaire also worried that Dawn's crying would damage her eyes further and that she would develop some other syndromes, making her health issue more complicated. It was a dreadful feeling for Blaire, a mother, and all of us to see a blind child helplessly crying, and we were utterly stranded and disheartened to convey our heartfelt concern and soothe her.

It was the most crucial ten days until we met Dr. Zee Herald. It was snowing heavily, almost like a blizzard, on the day of the appointment, but we needed to reach North Chester Hospital, north of New York City. By the grace of God, our traveling was smooth. The weather was worsening, and it was snowing heavily. We were under heavy stress and tension, but Dawn was silently sleeping and comfortable, and by the time we reached the hospital, and our turn came to meet Dr. Zee, we hoped she would not be cranky.

We never wanted to miss an opportunity to see Dr. Zee, as scheduling another would be critical once we missed an appointment. Dr. Zee's specialization was in congenital eye issues. He was an authority, and we were optimistic about resolving Dawn's vision issues.

While driving and heading towards the hospital, I saw a scene of three-dimensional snowfall effects as if we were traveling to some cloudland, a dreamland area. It had been snowing since the previous day. The wipers were ineffective, and Ryan had to drive with blurred vision. As Dawn was sleeping, there was nothing much to do but pray to God that we could reach the hospital safely and on time.

With such a backdrop, the three-dimensional snowing effect was becoming magnificent. Observing nature and expressing gratification was natural. Moreover, looking at the tense situation, I informed the others to keep them diverted.

Looking at the scene, everyone responded, saying, "Wow!"

We all could enjoy such a beautiful natural scene for a few more minutes, considering it a good omen, hoping today's meeting with Dr. Zee would be fruitful.

Somehow, we reached the hospital with many difficulties. We had started our drive an hour earlier than scheduled, as that was a good phase for Dawn, and also considering the severe weather conditions. After completing preliminary registration, we had to wait in the waiting lounge for the doctor's call. We all were anxious and had trepidation about the doctor's examination and conclusions.

It was fortunate that Dawn had remained quiet as usual during such morning sessions, as she used to cry heavily for long hours at night. Dawn had a good sleep in the waiting lounge; however, she called for some time, but it was manageable.

We wanted Dawn to follow her sleeping schedule so the doctor could check her eyes thoroughly and Blaire could ask questions to get complete clarity.

Dr. Zee came personally into the lobby to call Dawn's name. We saw him as senior and experienced, and we felt satisfied that we were in good hands.

He went through all the reports and also examined Dawn. With his many years of experience, he could conclude that Dawn needed cornea transplantation surgery and stated that Dawn would get vision.

It was like seeing rays of dawn. Our excitement and inner happiness were unimaginable. We all remained speechless for moments and then felt relaxed as if God had appeared in Dr. Zee to bless Dawn.

The doctor further clarified, "Yes, Dawn will be able to see her mother and the beautiful and magnificent world."

His statement was full of confidence, encouraging us, and we came out of the dusk, the deep despair, and saw rays of light. We started dreaming of Dawn happily playing with us and responding as if what we had gone through for so many days was an illusion, just a bad dream.

Dr. Zee also discussed the need for a cornea donor. He explained the long waiting time to get an organ donor but clarified that Dawn needed transplantation within three months and that he would try to put Dawn on a priority list and do the needful accordingly.

Dr. Zee explained to Blaire the basics of organ transplantation. He prescribed certain eye drops and other medication. He also suggested taking precautions so her eyes don't get infected before a cornea donor is available so that he would be able to do the transplantation surgery.

Blaire and the doctor discussed the issues in great detail. Blaire was thoroughly ready with questions, and Dr. Zee patiently replied and gave all the required information to Blaire's satisfaction. It was a great relief that Dawn would see her parents, grandparents, and this wonderful world, and she would not be blind.

The meeting with Dr. Zee was significant, and we all were satisfied with his opinion that if transplantation remained successful, Dawn would be able to see the world. He also tentatively said that the date would be in February, and we calculated that it would be almost the end of the fourth month from her birth. We had no option but to say yes, and Dr. Zee's meeting was over. It was a considerable consolation to all of us as we returned home.

We had several discussions while returning home. It was vital to see that Dawn's eyes should not get infected during such a lengthy period, and she should not develop any severe syndromes connected to her congenital issues. We all were worried, as her panicky crying problem was yet to resolve.

Dawn was not getting any relief from the medication, and her panicky crying was the issue. We all jointly committed and assured Blaire that what may come, we would take care of Dawn until she gets operated on for her cornea transplantation. The ninety days after that were crucial, like playing with a double-edged sword.

The worst and most painful part for everyone was that Dawn would remain blind until cornea transplantation surgery and the uncertainty of getting a vision. It was like passing through an unknown scary dark tunnel to see a ray of light, the *dawn in Dawn's life*.

The first twelve months would be most crucial for considering successful transplantation. Moreover, the initial formative developmental years meant the first six to eight years would be the most critical. Blaire knew that Dawn's problems would not end even after transplanting the cornea. If she developed poor vision, it would affect many more areas of her overall development. She might show up with related syndromes.

We all knew that Dawn would need close observation, supervision, and support for many more years. We knew we needed to follow the scheduled eye drops religiously and dutifully. Her eyes needed lots of care to avoid infections. She would need the drops for ten to fifteen years of her life and would have to continue to follow the schedule.

Blaire could not remain home for all those years, as she was a prime earner, and her income was crucial for their livelihood. Blaire realized that Dawn would need constant and close care, and she saw her mom and dad ready to support her in this challenging mission. She had the satisfaction of having safe hands to replace herself for Dawn.

Looking at her parents' trusted, reliable, and committed backup support relieved Blaire's tension, and she could breathe deeply to thank God. Blaire felt her motherhood and rejuvenated herself with caring, lovely compassion to do her best for Dawn and was entirely satisfied with such a condition.

Dawn got the vision, of course, with powered glasses and lots of instruction to take care of, and she was growing routinely without significant issues.

After the cornea transplant, it was crucial to take all necessary care of Dawn for the transplant to come out successfully, and by grace, we all could pass through the most vital phase of life.

Dawn had to pass through perceptive, reasoning, intellectual, social, emotional, and physical development. Of course, she did so under Blaire's direct control, guidance, supervision, and full support and protection.

Parents can nurture and nourish essential life values in their children by maintaining intimate harmony and dedication to perform persistently. They can also visualize a full-grown future person during those formative developmental ages with increased probabilities of traits like love, care, and compassion.

It was critical during such a stage that Blaire receive assurances without being explicitly told by Dawn, as she had responded persistently to all her guidance and training. Parents must perform their required duties and responsibilities and create a solid foundation by nurturing and nourishing life values within the child.

There is a thin demarcating line between sole responsible for the most relevant job and support and assistance while bringing up any child, especially when a child has congenital anomalies or life-terminating diseases. The mother may intuitively listen to her baby; the child also uses her senses and expresses urges and desires.

These senses are very useful for a child to understand parents and their personalities as role models. The child also becomes an intelligent observer and listener.

It becomes an obligatory responsibility for the parents to take special care and perform, so they do not have to repent looking at their child in the future. Typically, personality traits like talking, behaving, and manipulating develop in children based on the parents' characteristics. In conclusion, raising children can be simplified by becoming a role model, an excellent example for your children to follow.

In mid-2022, Dawn completed twelve years plus. She is a beautiful, charming, and sweet-looking girl who does all her routines as an average child does. She can see, read, speak, count, and sing and has a sharp memory. Dawn is meticulously intelligent and organized in all her routines.

She is a playing, dancing, cheerful girl, even at school. She believes in her mom, Blaire, and takes her mom as the final authority for any decision. Blaire has developed an excellent status as a guide and philosopher, and Dawn follows all her instructions.

09

Transmit Feelings of Parity
Shared Humility - Practicing Compassion

Compassion is an essential human trait with profound psychological and evolutionary roots and the most powerful tool that has played a significant role in ancient civilizations and continues to play in present-day families.

Compassion has many aspects in terms of religion and culture. Scientists have tried to understand the feeling of compassion scientifically through biological studies. They studied activities like heart rates and the secretion of bonding hormones like oxytocin in the average healthy person. They have simultaneously explored the working of vagus nerves in the brain's other regions with various activities.

Homeostasis, as currently defined, is an automated, self-regulated process by which the biological system maintains stability and remains adjusted to changed external conditions.

Endocrine glands secrete hormones into the bloodstream to maintain homeostasis and regulate metabolism in the body. The hypothalamus and a pituitary gland are command and control centers directing hormones to other glands throughout the body.

In general, homeostasis is a self-governing process of compensating for different environmental changes. It maintains body temperature, glucose, pH level, osmoregulation calcium, potassium, blood pressure, and many more through homeostasis. If homeostasis fails, the result is disaster or death.

The Oxford Handbook of Compassion Science[3] is the first academic book on the science of compassion to date. Scientists have applied their knowledge of psychology and sociology and their experimental observations to determine that a person can be challenged, provoked, and confronted by others' sufferings and misfortunes. Additionally, a person gets motivated to make the suffering person comfortable and see the possibilities to relieve him from his pains and sorrows.

Compassion makes a person aware of another person's suffering, empathizes with the person, and takes positive actions to alleviate such suffering. In similar aspects, one can see how people with congenital disabilities

---

3. Emma M. Seppälä, Emiliana Simon-Thomas, Stephanie L. Brown, Monica C. Worline, C. Daryl Cameron, and James R. Doty, *The Oxford Handbook of Compassion Science* (Oxford: Oxford University Press, 2017), https://www.oxfordhandbooks.com/view/10.1093/oxfordhb/9780190464684.001.0001/oxfordhb-9780190464684.

do not feel sad even looking at their shortcomings.[4] Much research is going on to explore compassion with the human mind and heart through neuroscience, psychology, literature, spirituality, and theology, which may be significant to the very survival of humankind and the environment we share with our entire existence.[5]

The naturally distinctive children having characteristics as differently abled can lead a contemplative life as observers, onlookers, and implied navigators. They become catalysts to create explicit passages to restore love, care, and compassion in the beautiful world, balancing intolerance, hatred, fanaticism, and loathing. It is not the only way to transform and establish a beautiful world filled with caring persons; however, it can be an excellent way.

They act as catalysts, meaning their presence and activities create a bond between two persons without being affected and disbursed. The parents otherwise also have natural bonding between them and their children. Their presence itself triggers accelerated changes to become compassionate. Please, do not show gloomy dejection towards children, which inhibits their unique characteristic of activating the heart-core emotions of their parents and other caretakers. It may disrupt their working as receptors, observers, and navigators.

---

4. Resources on compassion: the Greater Good Science Center at the University of California, Berkeley, https://ggsc.berkeley.edu/who_we_are/about; the Center for Compassion and Altruism Research and Education, http://ccare.stanford.edu/research/current-research/; and Sara Schairer, "5 Revealing Studies on Compassion," Chopra, June 13, 2018, https://chopra.com/articles/5-revealing-studies-into-compassion.

5 The Greater good science center at Berkeley, University of California, studied the neuroscience of well-being, sociology, and psychology.

It is essential to activate and enhance the process, and such catalytic agents should not become inert, uninterested, or unmotivated. Otherwise, the beautiful process of inspiring parents and other connected persons to be humane through the autonomous, sovereign system will get repressed.

Having an association with such a child is an opportunity and a boon. It is to get an endorsement of human beings' reaffirmation and reassurances of being humane. Once the parents and immediate family members accept the implied offer and act appropriately, they will start feeling the transformation within themselves. They can experience blissfulness and contentment while caring for such children.

It is obligatory to care for and love all children, as they come only at their parents' invitation. It is imperative to understand that they have particular characteristics and inherited traits from their parents. Hence, caring for and loving them with a reliable, unwavering sense of commitment is obligatory.

It is not the only way to transform and establish a beautiful world filled with caring, compassionate persons; however, it can be one of the excellent ways.

While taking care of them, please do not give feelings of kindness and generosity; show pity and mercy while caring for such children. Please, treat them with developed understanding and inner core concerns, and remain motivated and inspired to be on the path by being compassionate.

Parents must understand, appreciate, and accept that such children may or may not exhibit gratitude, so they should develop endurance, resolution, and broad-mindedness. However, do not forget to evaluate positively for benefiting self-transformation as an undeniable reward. If we look with a bit of wisdom and broad thinking, we will find a win-win situation.

We find distinctive children within the different types of families in every corner of the world without barring race, religion, caste, creed, wealthy or low-income families, and literate or illiterate to spread a sense of love, care, and understanding.

Differently talented children can also lead better lives through grouping and teaming therapeutic, curative medical trainers and caretakers, medical doctors, nurses, private tutorials, and even school teachers. Subsequently, these can also create a chain. Whoever comes into contact with already transformed empathetic persons and naturally distinctive children cum observers will be motivated further for societal and communal unity and harmony.

As discussed, compassion is not a relationship between the caretaker and the sufferer. Compassion is a deeply rooted perception in our human awareness. Until parents and dedicated family members realize their child's difficulties and pains as their own, they cannot perform compassionately and score to get upgraded.

It is natural for parents and immediate family members to feel disheartened and discouraged at the sudden arrival of differently-abled children in the family. However, when they sit and breathe peacefully, their consciousness stimulates their core values of being lovely and compassionate. Having developed serenity and blissfulness and having parenthood and motherhood feelings, looking at the child, they realize their child needs genuine devotion to obligatory responsibilities.

Compassion can be more effective today when we have audio, video, and print media that exhibit news daily from all over the globe on natural calamities and man-created disasters. Furthermore, we see commercials on TV from social service agencies, NGOs, and many more associations welcoming people to share their participation with naturally distinctive and orphan children under the shared humanity to harness community builders.

Compassion and letting the mind and heart develop empathy while observing beautiful nature are essential. Practicing lovely kindness and care for the needy in day-to-day life is the best way to learn to be a compassionate person. Dawn needed to create a beautiful, tender, lovely heart; there is nothing like practicing compassion in routine life incidents. We can remain motivated while handling distinctive children if we remain aware and awake of all minor-looking incidents and happenings routinely occurring in our existence.

Whenever possible, everyone should share their stories in a most natural and friendly way to draw the attention of others. It is the most straightforward way one can teach to be a compassionate person.

It is essential for parents and immediate family members to behave and pretend that they also have similar challenges and problems to transmit feelings of equality to the child. Sharing the overall sensation of being okay with having some shortcomings encourages such children and soothes them, as those are not severe issues as they may feel.

Dawn has a charming look with one displaced tooth in front of her jawline. She used to feel happy with such admiration for being a beautiful girl, and we could see the appreciation glow on her face. Similarly, boys can exhibit skills by jumping, climbing trees, and even playing and twisting their body joints.

Unless one develops compassion by feeling pain and suffering just by being with them, one cannot understand the naturally distinctive child's situation. It is essential to communicate those relations are between equals and not otherwise, and it must come out as shared humanity.

As discussed, a home having a distinctively-able child becomes a school for parents and immediate family members. Similarly, residential home communities can be places to practice compassion.

Dawn may not understand empathy, but the activity becomes interesting for her. We always invite her for a walk or stroll, and she happily joins us. Youngsters may not like activities like going for a walk the way older people do, but we could encourage Dawn to join, as she enjoys her grandpa talking to her about practicing compassion.

These days, Dawn has developed a beautiful, affectionate, lovely heart. Now she finds opportunities as soon as she comes out of the home to invite grandpa to perform attractive, loving, caring activities and feel happy.

Seeing turtle babies around the wooded area is expected since the community has beautiful lakes and ponds. It is usual to find turtles' babies moving around grassy areas during their breeding season. Some turtle babies lose navigation and come up to the residential community's walkways and even on roads.

It was an enjoyable activity to redirect those babies to their territories, water, and grass to save them during the walk and from being crushed under cars. It was nice to discuss and correlate how Dawn is happy to return from school to home, similar to what these babies may be experiencing.

Sometimes, a butterfly comes inside the room from some open door or window but then keeps dashing against the glass windows trying to find her way out, and one finds that the butterfly ultimately gets injured and nervously falls on the rim of the window. We had an opportunity to perform the role of rescuers to such a butterfly. It was fun for Dawn to pick up the butterfly through a small transparent plastic jar and release it back to the open-air area outside the home.

We remained astonished as the rescued butterfly flew plant to plant, came back flying very close to us, and took one round around us as if to say "thank you." We had a beautiful experience, and that was the most beautiful reaction of the butterfly.

Dawn was happy, clapping with excitement, looking at the scene after we understood how the butterfly acted compassionately. It was complete satisfaction and happiness for us to rescue the butterfly and see her flying back into her territory and enjoying the flowers' nectar. It was an extraordinary scene that left us stunned, with dropped jaws. Dawn's happiness and inner joy were apparent as she watched the butterfly until it disappeared from our vision.

Sometimes we would find a beetle lying on its back, upside down, and we found it struggling to be on its feet. So we gave a soft push to turn it and felt happy seeing it flying away.

As discussed, we all need to develop the habit of practicing compassion in day-to-day incidents. Practicing empathy can be an undying activity, looking at the vastness of nature. It is rejuvenating and refreshing every time to such a child, and looking at the joy and happiness of the one who accompanies them can also rejuvenate. The family needs to create lovely and caring behaviors to remain charged with performing responsibilities untiringly toward their challenged children.

It will not be misplaced to say that some ordinary-looking incidents can make understanding vibrant, exciting, and acceptable when someone wants to justify handling such children. It does not matter where we go; I always enjoy coming out with a passionate way of associating with Dawn about being caring and lovely to nature.

Finding earthworms and small lizards on the walkway is typical in Florida, and it has become a passion for looking for opportunities. While walking on walkways, we avoid stepping on those tiny creatures. Sometimes, we observe earthworms raising more than 30 percent of their body as if conveying they are misplaced, the lost way home, and looking for help to get back home to the grassland seeking rescue.

Dawn has started understanding such minor-looking compassion-signaling feelings. It was so satisfying when Dawn came out with a suggestion to help earthworms back to the grass area. Once we completed our job of pushing the worms back to the homeland grassy area, and after walking a few steps ahead on our way, Dawn thought of stopping and wanted to turn around.

She said, "Grandpa, how about we say enjoy and a bye to our rescued earthworms?"

Seeing a welcoming gesture on her face toward the rescued worms was a great reaction. We happily turned back and were about to greet those worms, but unfortunately, a bird landed at that spot and picked it up, and we saw the bird flying away. Dawn felt discouraged, nervous, and unhappy. She even cursed the bird.

It was an utterly annoying scene for her. However, I thought to explain further to Dawn so she would never get dejected and refrain from doing acts of rescuing such creatures in the future.

"Look, Dawn, do not get disappointed with such an incident. The earthworm must have felt good when we transferred it back to its terrain, but think about the bird. The bird may have babies in her nest; those babies need food and feel hungry like you. Just like mom serves you the food of your choice, this birdy mom must feed her babies."

However, this was not convincing to Dawn, as she had rescued the worm. Before Dawn remained in confusion, it was necessary to explain to her in detail about the food chain system in nature. "The worm we saw on the cemented walkway may have felt anxiety and fear of being lost from its habitat, and when we transferred it to its home back in the grassy area, it may have felt happy and relaxed. After reaching home, the comfort zone, it must have lived in a better mood for some time, and a better mood is a good healthy sign for any life."

"The bird wanted food for her babies, and if the bird had picked the frightened worm for her babies, her babies might not have received healthy nutrients. However, when birdy picks food from the grass area, she can feed better-quality food to her babies."

Still, this was not convincing to Dawn. Nevertheless, I could see her with a compromised understanding, so I told her, "Dawn, next time, you can act a little smartly and cleverly. Instead of placing the rescued worm or insect out in the open, put it in a safer place so birdy cannot find it."

Moreover, she said, "No, Grandpa, it was fine, what you explained." She added, "We did an excellent job for earthworms by sending them back home and making them feel happy."

Dawn also agreed and realized as justified birdy's picking up those earthworms for her babies to feed them. We expressed mixed feelings toward each other, and it was a great day seeing Dawn understand compassionately.

The earthworms do not have acute senses like other birds and animals to feel emotions, but those are the most protein-rich foods for birds and are the favorite food for American Robins. It was essential to clarify Dawn's doubts and see that she did not withdraw from doing similar acts.

After reaching home, to make Dawn comfortable, I explained the requirement for healthy food for every life on the planet. Healthy food is essential for having better babies. I told her about the food chain and not to lose kind-heartedness and attention towards small insects and worms. Humans are highly evolved lives on the planet, and it becomes our responsibility toward other lives, plants, and the entire existence of nature, to act compassionately.

I also reminded her about small signboards when we recently visited Utah, Arizona, and Colorado for tiny plant babies growing out from deserted sandy terrain. She had acknowledged by saying, "Yes, grandpa."

She had seen the placards and signboards saying, "Watch your feet; small babies are growing." I had satisfaction as grandpa explained things to Dawn, the granddaughter.

There are always reasons for every existence. We must transmit feelings of love, care, and compassion to the coming generation by being compassionate ourselves. They will enter the different competitive fields sooner or later, and we must teach them to handle and act moderately so as not to hurt or harm others and even get hurt, remaining self-centered.

Moreover, I narrated the instant of dawn's cousin, Molly, who always used to get an A grade ranking almost first in her primary school classes, but one day she cried after coming home from school. Luckily, Dawn was present on that day. I pacified Molly and had known the entire story from her, so Dawn could also understand. She got the third rank in some competitive exams, and while communicating with us, she blended with her disliking towards her classmates, who got first and second grades.

Dawn was also upset looking at the scene, and then I explained Dawn's cousin in her presence,

"Whenever she got the first rank, she was thrilled, but those two who had got second and third rank must have felt terrible and gloomy. They must have done better in the competition this time and deserved to get first and second rank."

Dawn's cousin had replied, "Yes, grandpa, whenever she was getting the first rank, her friends were feeling nervous and unhappy, but they congratulated her."

Furthermore, Dawn and her cousin understood that whoever works hard can get a better rank, but one should not show unhappiness and bitterness when someone receives the fruits of their hard work. It may also happen that someone may have a bit weak memory. Likewise, Molly had promised me that she would hug and congratulate them the next day. It was an excellent lesson for Molly and Dawn too.

Subsequently, it can also create a chain: whoever comes into contact with already transformed empathetic persons will motivate further for societal and communal unity and harmony. I humbly appeal to parents and connected immediate family members and all others as teammates to take an opportunity and offer services to naturally distinctive children. During their services, they must perform full-heartedly to explore and develop positivity to trigger differently-abled children's potential and ultimately qualify as righteous and worthy with pleasing complacency.

There are many inviting, enticing ways to be unethical and immoral by being uncivilized, antisocial, and even inhumane. Some of us can become addicted to drugs, alcohol, and even unreasonable desires and demands.

At the same time, this magnificent world offers many opportunities to be sincere, honest, caring, loving, and compassionate within human communities and throughout our entire existence. The arrival of naturally distinctive children is one of the natural routes to take an opportunity to improve and upgrade for a better life.

Whenever possible, everyone should share their stories in a most natural and friendly way to draw the attention of others. It is the most straightforward way one can teach to be a compassionate person. As conveyed, to make people aware, one can always share links, photographs, and powerful video clips through their short stories to make people aware.

Every religion has a segment, a group of religious adherents with misunderstood, misinterpreted, and misconceived beliefs and ideas. Dharmic religious supporters believe in the theory of rebirth and karmas, which has many beautiful core values. However, in Dharmic religious followers also have misunderstood, misinterpreted, and misconceived ideas about such children. Their sacred religious literature cannot be wrong, and no religious holy literature can be harmful, having bad ideas or misguiding the followers.

Dharmic religious followers must understand that children born with congenital anomalies or developing life-terminating diseases do not take birth in this world to complete their payback and sufferings. It is typical for some people to think that children with congenital malformations are born to suffer from such conditions.

Some of the adherents believe that their suffering is the consequence of wrongs they committed in their previous life or their parents saved them. However, it does not mean challenging the belief in rebirth and karma of Dharmic religions. In context with the subject of distinctive children, children taking birth with congenital anomalies do not make mistakes by knowing them as wrongdoers and sufferers; and even consider them as having come to complete their punishment.

We always do the prayers to admire and appreciate God as lovely, caring, and compassionate. It is to understand that no supreme God, almighty God, would like to create any life to suffer. It is we who commit wrongs, and in turn, we suffer. Understand it is what we make vibration, the energy we create, flow in the atmosphere will come back sooner or later, as we always remain busy to follow the same to see how it affects the targeted life. It is produced not outside but within the body, using one own energy to transmit to another body, transferring from life to life.

The created vibration, energy, will find the mother source if not consumed as it could not enter into the shield of the targeted body of serene aura, having sound vibration. At the same time, vibration and energy find their originating source center and will return. If such emitted energy successfully develops as targeted effects like anguish, dismay, pain, and suffering in some other targeted body, it may also return home merging, matching vibrations. The mother source center has remained active and involved and even comes near the powerful peripheral circle boundary to see how much it has affected.

Similarly, good sound vibration and its energy can influence the targeted body and may bounce back and return to the mother source center sooner or later, giving serenity and satisfaction.

We may understand the bounce-back, boomerang, and reverberating effects as destiny in the broader, wide-ranging sense. How can God think of punishing anyone who has just been born and has not been able to create any karmas (deeds), only remain involved to search and to match his vibration with his mother's lovely, caring, compassionate vibrations? Once any woman bears a child and becomes a mother by delivering a baby, she becomes different means loving, caring and compassionate woman. We believe in God and know Him as kind, loving, caring, pardoning, and forgiving; how can God punish the newly born child?

Scientists are working hard through their research to understand and succeed in eliminating the causes of children born with congenital anomalies and alleviating life-threatening, life-terminating diseases developing in children after birth.

However, to our experiences, new issues keep erupting from time to time, and consequently, the process may continue until this world establishes peace and harmony among people.

Moreover, there are self-governing, autonomous, self-operating systems for balancing human life values to remind us to be lovely and caring and live with compassionate feelings. And it is all time requirement of any human community.

Coronaviruses and their variants have recently made us believe in an autonomous, self-governing natural balancing system. Scientists could find vaccines to control suffering and death; however, many variants raised fears and anxieties.

Lord Abraham, Moses, Lord Jesus, Lord Rama, Krishna, Buddha, and Prophet Muhammad, followed by many Saints, Sufi saints, and Rishis, have suffered rescuing people from their despairs.

Lord Jesus appeared in this world, took away our sins, and suffered for us. He was crucified but reappeared after three days in front of His disciples to give them confidence that He was fine and the message that He was the Son of God. He even pardoned those who had done wrong to Him. Thus, in context with the subject, Jesus came for a specific purpose for the people by teaming actions to make everyone understand love, care, and compassion and find a doorway to dawn to enjoy the realm of the supreme God, the Father.

Lord Buddha appeared as a great teacher and explained unhappiness, indicated reasons for sorrow and showed solutions to come out of the same. He also showed how to get enlightened and awakened to find the doorway to dawn and experience blissfulness. Lord Krishna played an essential role in teaching the theory of karma (deeds) to explain how to live a balanced, compassionate life. Even Prophet Muhammad awakened the people and brought the messages to complete submission to Allah by remaining benevolent.

Do not mistake children born with congenital anomalies for divines or gods. Moreover, not to compare them with saints or holy, devoted persons. In all these explanations, there is no intention to reach children born with congenital deformities and disabilities with divines or gods. There is no intention to compare the beliefs and faiths of different religions. Furthermore, there is no intention to reach messiahs, avatars, and prophets. The purpose is to pass on the message of love, care, and compassion, which are the core values of every religion, faith, holy, sacred communication, and literature.

10

Understand Pain and Suffering
Naturally Born Distinctive Children do not Suffer

It is essential to understand human life compared with other lives before we are ready for the takeaway message about parenting children born with congenital anomalies and those who develop life-threatening or terminating issues after birth.

Scientists, philosophers, and many more have learned from nature and its existence finding innovative ideas for people's comfort and convenience. The process has continued and may remain unending. It is a modest attempt to encourage parents and dedicated immediate family members to accept a child with congenital anomalies and a child developing life-threatening, life-terminating diseases.

It is a disheartening, discouraging situation over which we understand we do not have control. The assumption is drawn based on parents positively taking up a turning point. Whenever something unusual happens, and if we keep positive attitudes and vision, most of it will improve life. It is essential to keep faith and patience, and one will find doorways to dawn.

It is a process where inhuman, unethical, and immoral persons get filtered and discarded, those who may not be suitable for promotion. It is to understand that nothing happens that is insignificant in the world. Every life has a reason to visit this beautiful planet, and every occurrence has its explanation and purpose. The following illustrations are to facilitate and convey proper understanding.

Our lovely romantic poets of the earlier years had birds as a favorite subject for making beautiful poetry. Birds exhibit multiple colors and unique body features while dancing and singing. They have distinct behaviors, especially their lovely caring family lifestyle. They enjoy flying and gliding with their partner, and one can be fortunate to see them soaring as a family group. Producing their progeny starts from building a nest to laying eggs, hatching and nurturing babies, and caring until they become independent enough to fly and sustain life.

We hardly take the opportunity to observe them with their features and activities. Those fortunate have seen flamingo cranes flying, with arrow patterns for conserving energy and maybe a protective device for young babies and other weak birds. It is scenic to see them flying with the backdrop of the clear blue sky or sometimes with black clouds. Avian biologists have studied many migratory birds. Birds travel thousands of miles to avoid unfavorable severe weather conditions and find suitable terrain and territory to give birth to their babies and nurture and nourish them to fly home independently.

The documentary *March of the Penguins*, directed by Luc Jacquet, shows the yearly journey of emperor penguins of Antarctica to reach their ancestral breeding ground. It is a wonderfully documented film about how parents raise their babies in adverse weather conditions and circumstances.

It appears the life of the birds is happy, as they can fly in the sky and walk on the ground, sit on beautiful trees, and have lifetime leasing rights to eat and drink as per their choice. It appears they do not have severe challenges and enjoy life with complete freedom, but these are our illusions that they do not have to face issues and threats from nature and others.

Bird-watching is lovely. It is an excellent opportunity for anyone to listen to birds' chirpings in the morning, hear them singing, communicate with each other, and welcome the dawning. Birds face problems under the survival of the fittest and the struggle for existence, mainly through the food chain. They communicate with each other for the morning routines, as they would like to fly away one after another out of the nest to eat, drink, and collect food for babies.

Beautiful, delicate, and even tiny birds prefer to build new nests during every breeding season by selecting some safe and secure place to hatch eggs, protected from stormy weather conditions and predators like reptiles and scavenger birds. Most birds build a new nest every breeding season to find a safe and secure place. Only powerful predators like eagles, crows, and vultures sometimes repair and use old nests.

The parent birds nicely organize and share responsibilities between the two of them. After emerging, babies from the eggs have more issues, as babies keep giving different calls to their parents, increasing their risk of getting picked up by reptiles and predator birds.

After arranging the required food for the day, the second job is maintaining security vigilance. Sufficient nutrition to raise growing babies sometimes leads both parents to pick up food. These birds make all these arrangements meticulously, but they face terrible attacks from predators who usually want to pick up babies.

Once a predator knows about babies in the nest, it finds opportunities to attack the nest. The scene of delicate birds fighting back as rescuers to their babies by dashing with predators and ultimately pushing away those predators from their babies is worth observing.

In many instances, the predator is successful and takes away the babies. However, those tiny beautiful birds chase the predator for long distances to the best of their strength to rescue their babies, giving appalling calls. It is the tragic scene of parent birds and sometimes of a single parent who restlessly keeps fighting and keeps giving terrible calls to drive away predators and ask for help from a partner.

Having babies snatched from the nest in their presence and killed for food must be an agonizing scene for any parent birds, especially mother birds. It was a terrible and disturbing scene I have witnessed most of the time during their breeding seasons. However, they keep struggling positively to save their babies, and the process continues untiringly.

It is a typical scene when friends or acquaintances meet a family with a naturally distinctive child and, during their conversation, very casually inquire about the child who was born with congenital anomalies. While communicating about the child's health issues, they unintentionally make some comments and statements regarding a child's health and condition.

Outsiders may share their true loving emotional feelings with parents who have a child with issues. It may be their expression of support and consolation by being passionate and sentimental. However, it is also natural for some people to look into others' problems and be judgmental, and they may not find any apparent expressions.

Once in a while, it may also happen that the parents become prejudiced against such a person and may find it hurtful and humiliating. Even though words may not be meant as severe and not uttered with the wrong intention, however, the parents take it differently. Subsequently, the parents remain upset while answering and making further communication. Those friends who catch those reactions also realize and apologize by saying there was no intention to hurt or insult.

These incidents do not happen every time, but parents feel hurt and unhappy, prompting them to feel guilty about not having a typical, healthy child. It becomes so unfortunate that even after parting, both the parents and friends carry the awful taste of memories for an extended time.

Parents feel unhappy and unfortunate about having a naturally distinctive child in their lives. Understandably, coming out from dismay may not be easy for them, as the child always reminds them even if they want to divert their attention.

It becomes essential for parents to accept the realities and change their attitude toward living happily and caring for their children. Under the prevailing situation, they expect others to change their attitudes and communicate to comfort them when they meet an unreasonable demand. Instead of hoping others to improve and change, it is more rational and sensible to understand facts positively.

Parents take sufficient time to accept the facts of their child. Whenever parents feel hurt by some words or statements spoken by someone else in connection with their child, it is essential to remember the day parents felt disheartened and unhappy at the birth of a child with congenital anomalies.

Even after that, while bringing up the child, parents may have mood swings to feel remorse and misery. Many other factors may play essential roles, like disputes between husband and wife and job-related mild to severe issues that keep cropping up routinely, fostering nervousness and melancholy. Ultimately, it boils down to extra concern for the child's congenital health issues.

If parents remained focused, they might learn that their distinctive child has differently-abled skills, capacities, and capabilities as blessings in disguise than other typical children. Many achieve remarkable milestones, lowering spectators' jaws and making parents feel proud and happy.

However, for every public appreciation event, the backdrop of a child's abnormalities and disabilities are noticed by guests, and honorable invitees remind parents and push them into desolation. Of course, one can see parents' attempts to feel proud, but at the same time, it is also pretty evident to see mild gloom and misery on their faces.

It is better to understand another way to overcome such commonly occurring suffering situations, avoid miserable conditions, and go through depression.

If parents remain focused, they might learn that their distinctive child has different skills, capacities, and capabilities as blessings in disguise compared to other typical children. Many achieve remarkable milestones, lowering spectators' jaws and making parents feel proud and happy.

Stephen William Hawking was born on January 8, 1944, in the UK and died at the age of 76 on March 14, 2018, leaving two daughters and a son. His wife Jane married him in 1965. At 22, he was diagnosed with a rare motor neuron disease and given a few years to live. The illness left him in a wheelchair rest of his life, and he could not speak except through a voice synthesizer.

Speaking to BBC in 2002, his mother, Isabelle, described him as a "Very normal young man." She said, "He liked parties. He liked pretty girls – only pretty ones. He liked adventure and did, to the extent, like work."

He wrote a memoir in 2013 describing how he felt when diagnosed with motor neuron disease. He wrote, "I felt it was very unfair – why should this happen to me." At the time, I thought my life was over and that I would never realize the potential I felt I had. Nevertheless, fifty years later, I can be quietly satisfied with my life."

Stephen was an English theoretical physicist, cosmologist, and author who, at his death, was director of research at the Centre for Theological Cosmology at the University of Cambridge. Stephen worked on the origin and structure of the universe, Big Bang to Black holes, and discovered that black holes emit radiation. He also argued that the universe begins at an infinitely small and dense point with originality, uniqueness, and distinctiveness. He was one of the most brilliant theoretical physicists in history. Today his description is almost accepted by other scientists.

Jiya Rao, a thirteen-year autistic young girl, daughter of an Indian Nany officer, accomplished and has recently established a record for swimming 28.5 km in thirteen hours and ten minutes from Sri Lanka to India to create awareness about autism.

Jiya was diagnosed with an autism spectrum disorder (ASD) when she was two. Moreover, a doctor advised her father to apply repetitive knocking movements in water sports as therapy.

The world's fastest swimmer to swim across the Palk Strait. She achieved this during cyclone Asani was steeping in Andamans. She established a record as the youngest girl with ASD to swim in open water into the sea. She received a special award from Indian Prime Minister Narendra Modi in 2022, the highest award for Indian citizens below 18. His father commented that autism is not a barrier but is a boon to her daughter.

Our conscience always gives sincere signals and vibrations about what is good to do, but ultimately, we surrender to our desires and demands, and whatever we want, we get. It is not that unhappiness comes from outside only, and always others become instrumental in creating unfavorable situations and disturbances in our lives.

Most people want to express their sympathy and may not find appropriate words and sentences. Very few ignorantly create humiliating situations, as they may be disturbed in their lives for their reasons. Such persons may involuntarily and inadvertently raise problems that hurt the parents of a child suffering from congenital issues. We all know that one can only share with others what one has. The things one does not possess cannot be shared, even if one wishes.

Everyone knows that wrong acts are wrong, and those might boomerang and bounce back, and the effects might be painful. We understand someone can express sentimental feelings, maybe by remaining callous and heartless and becoming dramatic. Once parents understand a person's basic personality, they must take it easy and reciprocate nicely. Good behavior might touch a person's core values and realize mistakes that are not nasty to anyone.

The positive attitude stimulation by parents might work as a turning point for such uncaring persons, and there are chances that good vibrations of realization may come back for a child and parents. It will be a wonderful experience, and one can notice such changes.

Similarly, if we think the other way, parents reciprocate hatefulness against someone's hurting words and sentences. In that case, it may add to a person's personality, and parents may witness and experience stronger reverberating vibrations, expressions of curses, and evil wishes that bounce back to them and the child. And he will be activated to churn memories and vomit more curses for the child's parents after reaching home. Thus, for the child's parent, it will be like unintentionally giving air to the fire, and fire comes out, justifying its role.

It is a humble appeal to parents of a child with congenital anomalies not to invite unhappiness repeatedly by feeling bad about someone's acts or comments and responding or reciprocating to those persons. Parents ultimately receive and gather what they never wanted from others.

A child cannot realize all such back-and-forth vibrations due to disabilities. However, a child's receptive brain might catch such vibrations. As a discussed hypothesis, forwarding such information to a natural self-governing balancing system by a child may become a point of degrading for parents. Moreover, if we scrutinize and remain honest, we cannot ignore that parents may also develop reasons to dislike and feel the burden of having such a child. Maybe this happens rarely, but it does happen.

It is not an outsider; sometimes, parents unconsciously act and make comments within their home that demonstrate their inner feelings of disappointment and dismay at having such a child in their life. It is human nature to come out involuntarily by becoming sentimental with near and dear persons like friends, family members, or between husband and wife.

Some parents accept special children as their destiny and take care as an obligatory responsibility. Some take care by loving, caring, and by being compassionate. In short, some have feelings of unhappiness and keep cursing themselves. At such a stage, it is essential to understand that resentment and antipathy transfer as negative energy to such a child. When parents create any negative energy or vibration while handling such a child, that negativity reaches such a child. It will be like, why should anyone get negative energy twice, creating and suffering with negative energy within and, the second time, in the form of having it bounce back from the child a boomerang?

With many more probabilities, it is natural for parents to speak, comment, or express feelings of misfortune at having such a child during a casual-looking talk with friends and relatives. It may be out of frustration, having many other issues within the family, between husband and wife, and may be due to job-related issues, but those may adversely affect all concerned.

Children with congenital anomalies will subconsciously register those casual-looking expressions of parents in their receptive brains, whether that casual-looking talk concerns them. It does not matter whether those were noticed by friends and relatives present at such time or not. It may not process for analyses or comments but may become a point of annoyance for children, and the parents may feel troubled and disturbed as a side effect of their child's feelings.

To show their antipathy, hatred, intense dislike, and unhappiness, these children may feel like going away from such a place and express unpleasantness toward their parents. Sometimes, they may exhibit sudden annoyance and irritation and would like to go to their preferred home corner to be comfortable at their earmarked place. These are places, corners of the house, where the child's brain may connect with a natural self-governing balancing system to send and transmit their vibration.

With congenital issues, the child may be unable to see, speak, or hear, as these senses have not developed as expected by medical standards. Even the brain may not be able to analyze and sync such communication of their parents' implied rejecting hurt, but those get stored in the child's unconscious mind to be transmitted further, as discussed.

Children typically seek their parents' and caretakers' attention to fulfill their demands and desires. It is common for children to feel anger and annoyance over minor issues. They sometimes exhibit aggression to keep beneficiaries active and focused and allocate essential attention and time. We have discussed the hypothesis that children with congenital problems take birth, having some assigned jobs.

They may also seek their parents' and caretakers' attention by exhibiting annoyance and anger, so parents remain alertly motivated to achieve upliftment by being loving, caring, and compassionate to complete their assignments. They do not want parents and immediate family members to stay ignorant and diverted and lose any opportunity to score better. Their job is to indirectly activate and push such members to get selected for the final squad to ascend to a better life.

Parents must remain optimistic, happy, and warm-welcoming to understand their aims and purposes. Once parents and other caretakers take care of their derailment and fix it, these children find everything is okay with their exhibiting implied attention.

These children are born with assignments for prequalified team members, parents, and other caretakers. As discussed, they are nominated, observers and navigators. In other words, they can be considered *trainers and coaches* to motivate and navigate all the prequalified team members while remaining observers and witnesses.

These children may have a comparatively shorter life than normal human beings. However, after putting in their efforts and offering many opportunities, if team members remain negligent, such implied trainers may become helpless, and there will be no alternative but to disqualify them. The prequalified team members have reached such a stage, so it hardly happens that they fail and lose rare opportunities.

The comparison with other children creates problems and inadvertently causes family members and caretakers to play an adverse role against themselves. Children's observant souls will be affected and become polluted with vibrations, feelings of guilt, unhappiness, annoyance, and intolerance.

Their brains may not smartly analyze messages like other children. However, as discussed, their brains are like icebergs. A significant portion of the iceberg remains underwater; without such an unseen portion, the glittering tip of the iceberg may not exist. It will be a great mistake to consider the tip portion of the iceberg as the whole ice floating in oceans.

Likewise, the human brain has a significant portion that is unveiled and unexplored, and it may operate and function differently. Nothing happens or exists without its causes and reasons on this planet earth. The existence of the non-active portion of the brain doesn't remain useless just because we have no awareness. Moreover, we should not forget that every life has a reason to visit this beautiful planet. Every occurrence has its explanations and purposes, and nothing happens without reason.

With all other shortcomings, the non-developed brain may have a potent reception power to catch vibrations from outside, especially from parents and family members with naturally matched frequencies. With such characteristics, some of these children may feel uncomfortable. Parents and immediate family members need to accept the reality of having a child with congenital anomalies and not make comparisons with other children to feel unhappy.

The problem is not with parents when they see disabilities and deformities as painful. With reviewed understanding, children born with congenital anomalies do not suffer, as they are born like that. Parents compare with other typical children and feel unhappiness thinking their children suffer. However, they remain anguished and astonished to see their children suffer, which is a natural and obvious thing for parents to discern and differentiate.

Children born with disabilities and deformities find joy and happiness by remaining connected to their world, whether someone takes exceptional care of them or not. Most of the time, they stay in a blissful and happy mood. If anyone observes them interestingly and captivatingly, they will find such children remain connected and can be with their discrete world, maybe with the self-governing system, as they do not have many worldly connections. If parents or other team members are involved with such pure, innocent, blissful happiness, one may get linked, joined, and connected to experience a serene experience.

These children may not share their happy mood with outsiders but with their parents, mothers, and sometimes closely connected grandparents. They hardly suffer from their deformities or disabilities unless someone consciously or deliberately reminds them to feel so and says something hurtful to them. It is essential not to remind such children of their shortcomings and make them feel different. Even if someone indirectly reminds them, conveys their issues, and makes fun of them, they get annoyed, which may draw them to feel remorse and sadness.

Children with disabilities do not suffer, as they have been born like that, but we compare them with others and create problems. Parents and other caretakers sometimes express their disappointment and sympathy, thinking the child is suffering and feeling unfortunate. Only parents and other connected people suffer.

It is the status of the mind that determines this. It is not our intelligence; most suffering is on memories. We perceive what we analyze with our brains, storing all those as memories. If we honestly look at memories, we have held them as painful from day one of knowing about a child's congenital issues during pregnancy.

Minds produce stress, tension, anxiety, unhappiness, fear, and much more as memory products, but the same brain can also create acceptance and remain joyful. In short, children with congenital deformities do not suffer. Parents and other family members only suffer from expectations, desires, and demands and are not ready to accept such children.

Of course, one can use science and technology to custom their inbuilt energy and intelligence to make their life comfortable, but do not expect what they do not have.

It will be unfair to push them too much by any concerned persons, including parents, to make them like a typical child.

Some show stunning changes with little uplifting of their hidden strength, and their parents feel proud. Some do not want to show up, which does not mean they are completely disabled. Some want to live with their ways because of limitations, as everyone shows their parents' traits and ancestral genes, which they only have provided by giving birth.

Parents want to train their children and feel they adapt well to their ways of life, or they sometimes feel stunned because the child has come up with differently-abled powers, energies, and skills. It would not be out of place to understand that most parents do not get satisfaction and happiness as per their desires and demands even with routinely born healthy children. They suffer so heavily from the undesirable acts of their typical, normal son or daughter that some go into depression. Some parents are in the habit of taking credit for every good happening as their accomplishment.

It is essential to realize and understand more elaborately in the world of people that some find the material world, the societal world, everything to live in, while others find it unworthy and go for spiritual growth. Everyone differs, with adopted likes, dislikes, capabilities, and capacities.

Some may consider some subjects or activities excellent, and others may find the same bizarre. Some develop extraordinary passions, while others see that as a waste of time and drivel nonsense, laugh at those persons, and label them eccentric and unusual. However, they may not know what eccentric, strange-looking persons achieve and perform for their accomplishments.

Every life comes into this world with adequate powers and energy, but as we know, a significant portion remains unused, or we may not be aware of their connections and activities. Children with congenital anomalies may come out brilliantly, shading their shortcomings. Either their parents or trainers, teachers, therapists, or the children themselves may come to know they have unusual natural talents and skills.

We see a society of dwarf people living happily in their community, meeting and enjoying their life, and there are many more examples to understand. It is natural that they accept and welcome each other and live life with compassion, and the associating, correlating effect is complete. No one feels different, low, and awkward. The newly arrived child will also not find it as diverse and uncomfortable with his growth as a child sees his parents and other family members alike.

They naturally remain compassionate to each other and without ill feelings, living uplifted life within their communities. They have self-satisfaction, complacency, and inner joy to live without complaints and competition.

Parents and families have genetic malfunctioning issues transmitted to a child, and the child is born with deformities and disabilities similar to them. We also see parents with congenital malformations and disabilities give birth to children with similar problems, as natural grouping assemblage effects. Furthermore, such children will be admitted to special schools most of the time. Thus, naturally grouped people are programmed further through our societal systems. We can know all such types of grouping and clubbing as assemblage effects.

All such group members appear to be suffering from their family situations. However, they may feel comfortable and at ease in their routine life as they do not feel the difference between them. They have a likeness to other typical families within their communities. In medical terms, they all have genetic malfunctioning but do not carry the feeling of congenital health issues within the family community.

They hardly find their shortcomings compared to other families within their communities, so they rarely suffer. They feel they are just different; there is no issue, and to find parity with others having extra, they have no pain and unhappiness. They do not suffer looking at each other, as they mostly remain in the association and connected. There will be an overall acceptance, as all are at par for becoming concerned and having considerate feelings for each other.

Do not label those families as cursed. It is a unique natural arrangement, so they do not differentiate amongst themselves within the family or at school. All such agreements give them the ultimate reverse effect: no one is different and abnormal in each other's eyes in their small world of people, small people's world.

Children born with congenital deformities and disabilities, recognized as naturally distinctive children for such exploration, are for balancing love, care, and compassionate human values against anger, hostility, hatred, intolerance, and many more inhuman evils. The entire existence and every human life on earth is a divine creation, and naturally distinctive children are also part of the same. They are part of a system that balances life values and humanity through self-governing balancing systems similar to the weather, environmental, geographical, ecological, and many more natural balancing systems.

We need to understand our judiciary system and the analogy to understanding such working. The self-governing, self-operating balancing systems of nature operate independently but under God's provisions, requirements and guidelines.

We have local courts at town and county levels, high courts at the state level, and a Supreme Court for the final verdict. All these courts, including the Supreme Court, work on the constitution, a precious document based on beautiful talks and literature on ethical and moral values to maintain a harmonious, peaceful living. When someone escapes by hood working all these systems, the matter will go to the Supreme court for judgment, rewards, or punishments.

Our judicial court systems have special provisions for children and teenage youngsters. They are taken care of when they commit any offense or mistake because of their ignorance or lack of maturity. Furthermore, under the special provisions in the law, there will be reduced and not vigorous punishment for their offenses, and they have to go through required counseling, teachings, and therapies.

Children have just been born into this world and have not performed any deeds knowing or unknowingly. If we understand this correctly, how does God sanction such terrible punishments by letting them be born with deformities and disabilities? How can they commit any crime or sin?

The purpose of making the team with parents and closely connected people is to give them a direction to lead their lives humanely, thereby providing a ladder to climb up for upliftment in their lives and upgrade for better positioning in the afterlife and may get entitled to salvation. They neither take birth to complete their punishment nor come into this world to suffer.

Through religious and spiritual knowledge, we know that awarding salvation is the power and jurisdiction of the Supreme God. Distinctive children can provide a unique platform and an opportunity for concerned people. Parents or teammates have to decide to climb up or go down the ladder with their acts.

With such provision of the ladder, having special children in a family should not be *treated as a bounty* of being with them. All such connected persons have to work hard and earn to be qualified for a final and better position in the afterlife.

Furthermore, while describing their role, we have recognized them as implied observers, witnesses, onlookers, and navigators. They come with a special appearance and characteristic features and perform different functions.

They have not come to comment, criticize, or guide; their implied way is to inspire, stimulate, and kindle by remaining nonjudgmental. It inspires, encourages, and adopts a lovely, caring, and compassionate manner for parents, dedicated, steadfast immediate family members, teachers, trainers, and therapists, including doctors and hospital staff, while dealing with them.

Their beautiful smiles and innocent hugs will lead us to adopt stunning, caring, compassionate values, ascend and uplift life during present living, and maybe transcend the afterlife to salvation.

It is not exaggerating or overstating to say that all religious understanding should start with children and end with children. Every religion has talked about children as pure, holy, and innocent, like a god. We make them changed, different, as per our convenience. Understanding and learning a lesson is essential to have a lovely, reassuring smile from them.

It is vital to make our foundation platform strong. It is imperative to understand that if typical, routine children learn and grow with human values, most life issues of the unhappiness of our families and communities will reduce to a great extent with time. At the same time, we experienced some antisocial, self-centered persons who may push innocent children into undesirable activities for their benefit. They train them for the most brutal scenes of persecution and oppression, harassment and torture, and the killing of innocent people, especially children, and women.

It is worth understanding the role of naturally outstanding children as differently able under their role as observers and navigators. We should also understand that distinctive children hardly connect with worldly people. They remain observers and witnesses and feed their reports by being nonjudgmental.

They beautifully create a team of different persons, impliedly inviting them from various fields to uplift by being loving, caring, and compassionate during their present life. They also provide an opportunity to transcend by upgrading for the afterlife and salvation.

There is no intention to hurt the feeling of any religious adherents who may have different opinions and beliefs as per their faith. However, the complete scene creates a *miniature replica of Noah's ark* to travel to the most serene, tranquil, beautiful, heavenly destinations. Do not remain casual and careless, and do not miss the ship if you are fortunate enough to be a team member.

11

Stepping towards Doorway:
Discover the Entry to Eternal Contentment

While completing the memoir with the takeaway message, it would be good to end with a beautiful, derived life anecdote.

Christine and Jay were on a trip for a week. Unfortunately, they never inquired and had no idea about the tornado that might develop during their absence and create problems. The twister affected many areas, including the village where they had recently moved.

They had moved from the city to a village due to the sudden bad financial condition and heavy losses in the business. They had also faced issues from family to friends, health to wealth, and many unexpected, unforeseen hurtful experiences. During all such adverse days, they had remained optimistic that God would take care and once again open the doorway to a happy life. However, they remained grounded, accepted the challenges, remained persistent, maintained their life values, and never lost faith in God.

Looking at the scenario while driving home, they remained anxious, thinking about their house. The road to their home was not that bad and was drivable. As we reached the county, the traffic slowed down through the storm-affected areas. They passed through a few villages and saw that some homes had been entirely swept away into debris. They noticed many more houses in damaged conditions, with minor to significant damages.

By the time they reached their hometown, it was late evening. Fortunately, it was a full moon day, and they could see their house. Christine saw a half of the roof had blown off, and one of the corners of the home was severely damaged. She was anxious as the home needed extensive repairs.

After enjoying a high-end life for many years in the city, settling down in a village was painful. A daughter and sons were on their way to settle down their lives with their families. Jay had prepared her to leave the city life and return to their old residence situated in the village.

Looking at the home condition, they both got dejected and thought about how to manage repairs and resettle to live life. Fortunately, the ground floor of the house appeared not much affected; however, more than half of the roof of the upper floor had blown up from the bedroom side, damaging some part of the outer walls.

Christine was upset and nervous and refused to enter the home, as she believed she might not be able to withstand looking at the damage. Jay went inside the house to survey quickly about the catastrophe to inform her so she could prepare herself to endure the damaged condition of the home.

The moonlight was sufficient to reach the upper floor, half of the bedroom roof had blown off, and one of the walls had broken. The bathroom, wardrobes, and some other areas were entirely messed-up.

Jay never wanted Christine to look at the utterly haywire condition of the upper floor, especially the bedroom, so he removed some planks and debris, pushed the mess into the corner, and quickly cleared the bed area. However, the room was broken and opened to the sky.

While managing all these, Jay took some more time. Christine worried and gave a loud and clear call that she would also like to come up, and she reached the upper floor bedroom area. When Jay saw Christine enter the room, the most damaged portion of the house, he asked her to keep her courage and not to get upset and made her sit on the chair next to the bed to calm down. She had tears, thinking that the fixing might need lots of money, and she knew they had no big money left.

They had already exhausted driving in slow-moving traffic and remained worried before reaching their hometown. Looking at the scenes of many damaged homes on the way, they were anxiously concerned about their home conditions. She was almost disheartened and in a dismal state, so Jay thought to change her gloomy mood but then how?

To handle the situation and change her mood, Jay helplessly looked at the sky from the broken roof and saw many glittering stars, and the moon was in its grandeur. The storm had created a vast passage by breaking open a significant portion of the bedroom walls, allowing a nice breeze to calm down and soothe them, and he thought to change her mood.

Jay smiled at Christine, but she did not respond. He started whispering and singing in a husky voice, which broke her silence, but she was annoyed.

"Why are you acting so funny, Jay?" she uttered.

"How can you think of singing and making fun of this suffering situation?"

"Christine, do not be upset." Jay calmly spoke to her.

"They saw the entire scenario during their journey home. A few houses in their community have wholly blown off into debris. Some were severely damaged. Their house is an old house that would have blown up completely, but only half the roof has gone. They must thank God that half the rooftop has remained undamaged."

"They can still use their bedroom until they repair and fix their roof and complete other repairs. Be calm, relax, and look at the sky. They never had a chance to look at the vastness of the sky, with so many glittering stars and, on the other side, a full moon. These are rare opportunities."

Christine listened patiently to Jay and encouraged him to complete his talk.

"Christine, do you feel God has given them the excellent opportunity to look at His exceptional glorious existence by removing a portion of the roof?

"They hardly had any opportunity to look at the sky, glittering stars, and moon as they remained busy in their lives for so many years in a highly illuminated city. Even after they moved to this village home, they never thought of going for a stroll in the evening and have not enjoyed the village's peaceful, scanty illuminated area so far." Christine had calmed down by that time and comforted herself with gentle air blowing.

"If he had known earlier," Jay jokingly concluded, "He would have broken off half of the roof himself earlier. She must agree that looking at, perceiving, and witnessing beautiful nature is wonderful, and that was their passion too."

Christine smiled and said, "Jay, you are crazy."

She confirmed, "She never thought of it, but by the time she comprehensively encompassed the magnificent sky. It had escaped her attention about the wonderful and glorious sky scene through an enlarged window for gratification and appreciation."

She cherished Jay for making her feel happy and blissful and for reminding her how to take dreadful incidence lightly.

She understood God's message that when sudden unexpected painful circumstances develop in life, instead of frightening and discouraging, one needs to find an opportunity to review the situation, accept it as it is, and take up the challenge to change for a better understanding.

She threw herself on the bed and decided to sleep under the sky, looking at glittering stars and the full moon's glory, which had spread all over the bed through the broken roof.

Christine happily hugged and said, "Do not worry, Jay. We will fix the roof together." She agreed to the proposal to repair the roof and other home areas with firm support and harmony.

They enjoyed looking at each other, smiling, and whispering many assurances and lovely messages. Moreover, they understood that a relationship means to know each other well and gain confidence in each other.

Dawn, The Doorway

The career-oriented couples would like to put extra effort into their jobs to grow and get established to live a happy life with comforts and convenience. At the same time, they also would like to invite a child into their life to enhance their relationship, creating a lovely, blissful, perfect link between them.

However, sometimes a child is born with congenital lifelong enduring anomalies or develops a life-threatening terminal disease. It is natural for parents to feel terrible and think of shattering their dreams. Parents may feel disheartened and discouraged thinking about how to manage. Especially a mother who feels unhappy and downhearted can be understandable, natural, and acceptable. However, when the mother calms down, she realizes her obligatory duties and breathes peacefully.

Consider this a turning point for the better, and one may have to change the complete approach toward life. Perform your best to assist and find opportunities to lead a happy and blissful life together. Instead of remaining distressed, accept that everything that happens has some purpose. It will be better to start feeling transformation for a better life, leading to a higher stage of insight. The most gentle and blessed approach is to stay positive, perform their best sincerely, and move in the right direction by being virtuous and compassionate.

Have an option at every turning point to live happily, provided one is ready to accept and adapt to every new circumstance. One may go through a rough road and face difficulties if destined, but it may offer many opportunities to achieve higher goals. It is better to remain positive and find joy and satisfaction.

One may have to adapt, overcome challenges, and remain out of comparison and competition. Nothing is immortal and eternal, and everything has to go through the transformation process to support natural balancing systems.

Everyone has to pass through different phases of life, whether one wishes and wants it or not. Before birth, one goes through nine months of gestation in the mother's womb. Once a child is born, it has to pass through different phases of life, from childhood to a young adult phase, gaining the maturity to live an independent life, adult to senior-aged adult, old age, and death.

During the gestation period, along with all other body parts, and vital organs, the brain develops, and the ensoulment process also occurs. The fetus remains connected with the mother through the lifeline support, the placenta. The fetus remains dependent on the mother, from breathing to blood circulation, eating to excretion, etc.

It is the loveliest experience of life for the fetus. It is a state of just being, to be present. In other words, it may not be exaggerating to say it is a tranquil place to be within oneself.

After having enjoyed carefree, peaceful, effortless life within the mother's womb, nevertheless, after birth, human remains in search of peace and harmony at every stage of life, but the thirst never quenches. Whenever a mother gives birth to a child with congenital issues, the child behaves and lives carefree, which may have some connection with the hypothesis we discussed.

Spiritual and theological knowledge has provided a sufficient understanding of how to be happy and blissful, which different people have understood according to their faith beliefs. However, the core value explains having moderate demands and desires and living with happiness and contentment without harming and hurting others.

Our planet has enormous treasures of all different kinds. There are meticulous natural self-governing systems to keep all different types of balance in our bodies and the world. Every life starts at emergence, and survival requires growing to reach the predetermined, predestined pinnacle and then traveling through decline to complete life. To achieve our life purposes and aims, we have the opportunity to uplift life and to have an upgraded position to travel further.

We need to understand the basic principle of giving, which is the vibrant nature of our entire existence. There are more acts of giving than taking, which is how self-operating, self-governing autonomous systems balance and operate smoothly. However, most human beings have excluded themselves by not adopting the nature of giving effectively and have become hindrances in these self-operating systems.

Whenever a child is born with congenital deformities, parents and immediate family members suffer as they compare their child with others. It is typical for the parents to keep getting hurt and unhappy and suffer because their child is not doing something similar to others. Parents suffer because they compare with others routinely and feel their child is not on par with others.

Every life has to adapt and make necessary changes, known as adaptation, to survive. We know that naturally distinctive children have unveiled energy, power, and dynamism within, and if someone makes an admirable effort to initiate, they can also show excellent performance.

One is happy remaining in routine while the other is enjoying challenges. One who happens to be in an odd situation accepts it as fortune and destiny, while the other takes up the challenge to find a doorway to come out, maybe getting pain and suffering in others' eyes to gain contentment.

The prime purpose is an understanding that a naturally distinctive child born with characteristic abilities is to prepare and uplift well-performed parents and teammates for ascending the mystic ladder of divine spiritual life. They encourage creating an agreement, the bond between the parents and complete members of the team to unite and change and to become compassionate.

The parents have a distinctive child within the family who has an opportunity to dawn for uplifting. They lay a platform for the commencement of developing understanding and rising to score for upgrading.

They are the spring source; they trigger flow and buoyancy to parents and all concerned family members and teammates and invite them to plunge into their world of innocence and purity to rise with selfless love and compassion. They can also stimulate the doorway's opening, elevating caretakers to be humane during their present life in this world and for better placement in life after.

They come to inspire and draw parents and others, carrying lovely, dedicated souls to join as teammates toward the doorway to dawn. In other words, they come as differently-abled onlookers to initiate thresholds for the entrance to elevate human life. Sometimes the things we cannot change will end up changing us.

They come as expected, intended, and planned observers, so parents, single mothers, and immediate family members should not consider themselves unfortunate; on the contrary, they should remain more involved, dedicated, devoted, and compassionate while taking care of such children. Their emergence can be a part of the natural system, a self-operating balancing system discussed earlier in context with the subject.

They come so naturally that some people take them casually and make mistakes in recognizing them. They visit as specially designed and assigned jobs as distinguished onlookers, distinctive observers, and witnesses as balancing beings.

They indirectly provide a platform for parents and steadfast, committed, caring family members to prepare themselves to live with awareness, responsiveness, genuine compassion, and emotional dedication to perform obligatory responsibilities.

They also lead an austere, contemplative, reflective life as surveyors, explorers, and implied navigators. Their taking birth in the family can be considered a boon. It is to get an endorsement of human beings' reaffirmation and reassurances of being humane.

Once anyone accepts the offer as a boon and acts appropriately, they will jumpstart to feel the transformation and transcending from within themselves and experience blissfulness and fulfillment while caring for such children. They also become catalysts to create explicit passages to restore love, care, and compassion in the beautiful world.

For a family with a distinctive child, the home should become an everyday school to practice compassion, which is the most practical way. It will also indirectly be helpful for community building.

Writing a book on naturally distinctive children aims to draw parents and immediate family members to be especially virtuous, look a beam of light into such innocent hearts, and express privileged gratification to their interactive souls.

Believe it or not, it may also become an opportunity to ascend the mystic ladder of spiritual and divine life for better placement, which can be a blessing in disguise. It is an effort to explain that one can choose to be happy, as these children are distinctive, so it does not matter; they may or may not show changes and improvements against efforts put in, but look at how they change us by navigating the path of transformation.

Consequently, transformed persons become assets for other friends, relatives, and even the community by being humane and compassionate. The transformation of being benevolent itself is the most significant achievement as a blessing in disguise.

Last but not least, they provide an opportunity for lovely pets and specially allocated trained dogs to ascend the ladder and qualify as admirable and worthy guides and companions. The shared experiences of many people with their beautiful dogs have an exchange of pleasant, caring emotions blended with a high degree of loyalty, sincerity, and faithfulness.

Dogs maintain grace and dignity while walking alongside differently-abled children and people having congenital disabilities, which is splendidly admirable.

Pets are playful and joyful, giving us happiness and joy, but they are more than friends who share stress and tension. A dog's life is not as long as a human, but they establish a relationship in such a way that makes our life complete.

There are many real-life stories where dogs have become rescuers and are undoubtedly unconditionally great friends.

My next book is

LUCY, a lovely dog - *Sacrificed her life.*

J M Mody lives in Florida, USA. The backdrop of academic qualifications, graduation in biology, and master's with specialized subjects, Comparative Reproductive Physiology, and Behaviors, made him systematically analytical. He also has a legal law degree, which has sharpened him to understand pragmatically with logical reasons.
Visit him at www.jayeshmody.com

He has gone through many challenging situations in life, which have enriched him with enormous experiences, and he developed an appetite for writing to reach readers. A nature lover craves to understand routine happening unique natural events and develops a passion for remaining gratified.

Books published and available on
Amazon (Internationally), Barnes & Noble

EMPOWERED MOTHERS AS TRENDSETTERS

Intimate harmony to perform
persistently for earnest Accomplishment
YouTube: http://www.youtube.com/watch?v=eMcwM8RJyU8

"At this book's core is its view of the mother as the key player in family life. Mody's arguments are generally easy to follow." – **Kirkus Reviews**

"Mody… explores the importance of mothers in raising children by employing fiction and nonfiction. In the fictional sections, a single mother rescues a stranger's children in addition to her own from a village flood..." **Kirkus Reviews**

A well-intentioned…." – **Kirkus Reviews**

FORTHCOMING Books During 2023:

- ➢ VANGUARDS, A Present-day Rescuer
- ➢ LUCY, A Lovely Dog, Sacrificed her Life
- ➢ DIVYANGS, Do not know them as Disables
- ➢ COALESCE, Giving up Loyalty
- ➢ DON'T PANIC. Lead a Happy and Blissful Life

(Under REVIEW to come out with a REVISED RESTRUCTURED EDITION).
YouTube: https://www.youtube.com/watch?v=jk2ahmMif_0&t=17s